10 things
I wish someone had told me
about retirement

Rein Selles

Jim Yih

Patricia French

FIRST EDITION
Designed by Thumbprints Design Studio, St. Albert, Alberta, Canada
Printed on acid free paper

Library of Congress Catalogue-in-Publication Data
Rein Selles, Jim Yih, Patricia French.
TEN THINGS I WISH SOMEONE HAD TOLD ME ABOUT RETIREMENT / Rein Selles, Jim Yih, Patricia French. - 1st. ed.
p207 cm.
        ISBN 145057405X
        LCCN 1-4392-2045-X

Foreword

Professional Retirement Planner (PRP)

For many years, the concept of retirement planning in Canada had more to do with selling products than it did with helping people plan their future lifestyles. Today, retirement educators, financial planners, estate planners, risk managers, brokers, nurses and psychologists gather annually to explore how their individual areas of expertise might help others learn more about retirement planning.

For over 30 years, the Retirement Planning Association of Canada (RPAC) has promoted lifestyle planning as an integral part in the retirement planning process. The Association provides a multitude of resources to members and the general public using a variety of education programs.

Of particular interest to professionals working in the area of retirement planning in associated fields is the Professional Retirement Planner (PRP) designation. The designation ensures clients that they are working with an individual who has the relevant education, the experience and a high commitment to professional development in the field of retirement planning.

For further information on the Association or the PRP designation, please visit the RPAC website:

www.retirementplanners.ca

or contact the national office at:

RPAC National Office
289 Greenwood Dr.
Stratford, Ontario
N5A 7K6
(519) 273-5616

Rein Selles, MSc, PRP
Jim Yih, CSA, RDB, PRP
February, 2010

Professional Human Ecologist and Professional Home Economist (PHEc)

What do Professional Human Ecologists and Professional Home Economists have in common? They share a mandate to enhance the well being of individuals and families in daily life by helping them make the best use of their resources. In Alberta, Professional Human Ecologists and Professional Home Economists are university graduates working in a variety of fields such as business, social service, health care, education, policy, and financial counselling and planning. They have training and experience in money management, consumer education and behaviour, food and nutrition, housing, clothing and textiles, family dynamics, and human development.

As a science, Human Ecology evolved with a broader scope from the field of Home Economics, and shares a clearly defined framework to assist in practice, teaching, and research. Human Ecology is integrative and holistic and expands its scope of knowledge and practice beyond interactions within the home environment to include interactions with wider socio-cultural, economic, natural, technological, and global environments affecting people's daily lives.

The Alberta Human Ecology and Home Economics Association's (AHEA) proud history began in 1935. AHEA is registered under the Professional and Occupational Associations Registration Act (POARA) in Alberta and the Human Ecologist and Home Economist Regulation gives exclusive use of the titles Professional Human Ecologist and Professional Home Economist and the designation abbreviation of PHEc to those who are registered members of AHEA.

The PHEc designation represents commitment to ethical professional practice, competent and responsible service to employers, clients and the community at large, and maintenance of competency and ongoing professional development.

For further information on the Association or PHEc designation, links to other provincial, national and international associations, please visit the Alberta Human Ecology and Home Economics Association (AHEA) website:

www.ahea.ab.ca

For information on university programs for education in Human Ecology in Alberta, please visit the Department of Human Ecology, University of Alberta website:

http://www.hecol.ales.ualberta.ca

Patricia French, MSc, PHEc
February, 2010

Index

Foreword 3

Introduction 7

First Thing - Planning Is Personal.. 9
Round Table
    It's MY Retirement 13
    Chasing the Goals of Others 15
Making It Personal
    Exercise 1 17

Second Thing - You Cannot Retire from Yourself 19
Round Table
    Retirement - Your Dream Job!..................................... 27
    Making Retirement the Best Years of Your Life 29
Making It Personal
    Exercise 2 31
    Exercise 3 32

Third Thing -
Retirement Is More about Spending than Saving.................... 33
Round Table
    The Budget - Blasphemy? 43
    How Do You Know How Much to Save if You Don't
        Know How Much You Spend? 46
Making It Personal
    Exercise 4 49
    Exercise 5 50

Fourth Thing -
The Best Retirement Plan Is to Be Debt Free 51
Round Table
    When Debt Can Make the Heart Grow Fonder 67
    Is Debt Used for Investing a Good Form of Debt? 69
Making It Personal
    Exercise 6 72

Fifth Thing -
Investing IN Retirement Is Different from
   Investing FOR Retirement 75
Round Table
    Hindsight Is Perfect Planning!..................................... 86
    Goal Setting Your Retirement Savings........................... 88

Making It Personal
Exercise 7 91

Sixth Thing -
Insurance Is for the Living (and the Dead).............. **95**
Round Table
Insurance Planning Is a Good Rehearsal.................... 103
Insurance Should Be Bought - Not Sold..................... 105
Making It Personal
Exercise 8 107

Seventh Thing -
Paying Less Tax Is My Choice................................... **109**
Round Table
Tax and the Telephone 119
Tax "Myth" Information 121
Making It Personal
Exercise 9 125

Eighth Thing -
**Planning Your Income in Retirement is
Like a Treasure Hunt** **127**
Round Table
Learning to Turn On (and Off) the Taps 140
"Working" Your Retirement Income 142
Making It Personal
Exercise 10 146

Ninth Thing -
**Estate Planning – Better the Memories
than the Money** **151**
Round Table
Organizing Your Estate.. 160
Last Love Letter 165
Making It Personal
Exercise 11 169

Tenth Thing -
**You Are Already Retired.
The Problem is You're Working!** **171**
Round Table
Retirement Is a Life Within a Life 189
Hey, Can I Have a Do-Over?...................................... 193
Making It Personal
Exercise 12 197

Introduction

As teachers of retirement planning, we invite workshop participants to share in the learning experience by asking them to write out specific questions at the outset of every workshop. A question that comes up regularly is this one:

"What are the most common mistakes Canadians make in planning their retirement?"

Since people tend to learn more from their mistakes than their successes, the question prompted us to reflect on how one might look back on retirement, in perfect hindsight, to see what planning and activities should have been done.

Mistakes made in planning retirement often come about because of a lack of knowledge. Ironically, that knowledge is available but seems less relevant to most Canadians when work, family and personal goals are a priority. By the time motivation increases, some of the key choices a person could have made are no longer possible.

Course evaluations regularly state, *"I wish I had taken this course 20 years ago."* The reality is that the individuals who make this kind of observation likely wouldn't have taken the workshop because they were not ready. Are **you** ready to think about your future?

As professional planners, we will each focus our knowledge and experience in areas where we can make the greatest contribution to this book. The concepts we are passing on to you are the ones we think make the greatest difference between failure and success in retirement. We also recognize that while one of us may offer a specific idea, the rest of the team may have other points of view. We have included these insights at the end of each chapter in a "Round Table" discussion.

If you would like to know more about the authors, a brief biography is included at the end of the book (see pages 203-205). We welcome your comments and observations about the book.
Please write to us at:

Retirement/Life Challenge Ltd.
9 Elliot Place
St. Albert, Alberta, Canada
T8N 5S5

or via the Internet:

www.retirementchallenge.com

Notes

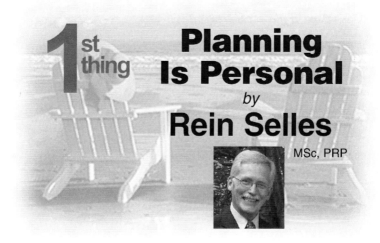

Planning Is Personal

by

Rein Selles

MSc, PRP

A workshop participant once asked me what I thought was the greatest obstacle to retirement planning. I felt then, as I do now, that most of us don't take the task personally. Polls measuring Canadian behaviours have indicated that people are reluctant to begin planning retirement. The problem was highlighted in **Insurance-Canada. ca's** web-site regarding the 2006 Desjardins Financial Security Survey:

> *"Canadians need to realize that retirement is not a 20 - or 30-year vacation,"* says **Monique Tremblay**, senior vice president of Savings and Segregated Funds for Desjardins Financial Security. *"People need to change their behaviours and start planning for retirement as soon as possible - earlier than the average age of 35 years old. It is understandable that the extent of the planning and saving must be in relation to the needs and financial capacity, but a simple plan is better than no plan at all,"* adds Tremblay. *"Retirement planning is not just about RRSP contributions. People also need to consider the social aspects of retirement and how that impacts their finances as well."*

TYPES OF PLANNERS

To establish a baseline for the nature of personal planning, I undertook a research project with assistance of a colleague, **Garry Keiller**. The study involved 400 respondents in Edmonton and measured both their planning behaviours and their relationship to professional advisors. In-depth interviews with a smaller sample gave some insight into how Canadians deal with retirement planning. The results indicated that the first step in planning was the raised awareness of the need to secure the future or *"Knowing"*. The descriptive data of our study showed three distinct groups of behaviours: those who were conscientious planners from an early age (life planners), those who began planning when their income rose to a level where tax planning became desirable to shelter income from tax (tax planners), and those who did minimal or no planning at all (no planners).

Life Planners were brought up to believe that planning, saving and budgeting are part of life. Life planners began saving with their first paycheque and have continued throughout their lives regardless of circumstances. These people benefited from advice as to investments but needed no motivation or encouragement to save. Life planners seemed to be the most security conscious of all the groups. They purchased life insurance, contributed to pension funds (where available) and preferred, what they perceived to be, low-risk investments.

> *"Financially I was always concerned. I was raised that way to look after myself. I've saved ever since my first pay cheque."*
> - A "LIFE PLANNER"

Tax Planners began saving as tax planning usually at the age of 35 to 40 when their incomes were increasing. These respondents were interested in advice regarding sheltering their money from tax and there was no particular focus on retirement planning. Many began with the purchase of Registered Retirement Savings Plans (RRSPs) and increased their contributions as they were able. Gradually, their investments grew and they were in a position to consider other types of investments.

> *"All my investments were purchased with tax planning in mind and not really retirement planning. It just turned out that way."*
> - A "TAX PLANNER"

In addition, tax planners often had careers with excellent benefits and pension plans as well as insurance through the workplace. Accumulated wealth was perceived as a retirement fund only when the individual began to consider the possibility of retiring.

No Planners lived their working lives from paycheque to paycheque. They may have had the benefit of pension funds through work but this was often the extent of their planning for the future. Although this group may still have believed savings were important, they felt that they were unable to save money because of the circumstances in their lives.

Many in this group believed that to begin financial planning one must have a substantial sum of money. They perceived that the purchase of an RRSP was an unattainable goal. Because no planners held this belief, they did not seek information regarding financial planning and they were uninformed about their options. The respondents in this group tended not to seek professional help because of the following perceived barriers:

1. They believed they could not afford professional advice.

2. They were embarrassed to reveal their ignorance in financial matters.

3. They felt professionals handled only large amounts of money and, therefore, respondents were embarrassed to reveal their incomes fearing ridicule, disrespect, or rejection from the professional.

No planners could also be caught off guard by retirement, especially forced early retirement, due to changing personal health or staff reductions at work.

"It is not a bed of roses when you are forced to retire early. I had a daughter to raise and there was no money to put away after mortgage payments and expenses. I could not afford RRSPs."
- A "No Planner"

RECOGNIZING BEHAVIOURS

Could you see yourself in any of the planning types? More than likely, if you are in a family, you could identify various members as having characteristics that match one or more of the types of planning behaviours presented. You may have noticed that respondents in the study used professional advisors in different ways. Life planners, in particular, tended to utilize professional resources to assist in obtaining information and advice. No planners, on the other hand, did not feel their financial positions warranted professional help - even when that help could have been critical to their own well being.

Ideally, people should be encouraged to plan and learn the skills of planning at an early age. In our research, however, respondents reported they were busy raising a family, paying off their homes, struggling in their career or business, and feeling that retirement was very far down the road. Many respondents said they wished they had begun planning earlier in life, but they believed they could not afford to put money away. What seemed to be missing was an assurance from their financial institutions and advisors that it is perfectly acceptable and worthwhile to begin saving with small amounts of money.

Respondents reported that the tactic of professionals which most negatively affected them was, *"arousing and playing upon guilt feelings."* Guilt was created when professionals indicated what the individuals should be doing (prescriptions) rather than helping them realize what could be accomplished (choices), given the personal circumstances they were in.

INTERNAL VERSUS EXTERNAL PLANNING

While personal behaviours shape the form that our planning takes, the responsibility for the outcome of the plan can still be a problem. Think, for example, of a couple where both make a decision to take out an investment loan. While the investment rises in value, the couple is happy. The moment the investment falls below the value of the loan, one turns to the other and says, *"This is all your fault!"* Those who plan personally not only take responsibility for creating the plan but they also accept accountability for the actions taken to bring the plan about.

External (Hands Off) Planning assigns responsibility and the accountability to others. While one may bring some goals to the table, it is one's partner or a professional that is assigned the task of bringing it about. When things don't turn out as expected, blame is quickly assigned. I don't believe that all external arrangements are necessarily wrong. When you are busy with work and family, working with an external planner may be very important to bringing about your plan.

Internal (Hands On) Planning is the foundation for personal planning. It has the following key characteristics:

~ You recognize that the plan comes from you, not from another.

~ You value input from others - whether family or professionals - but you understand that the decisions will need to come from yourself.

~ You may enjoy implementing plans but can also value and understand having others implement - provided you are kept informed.

~ When the outcomes are not what you expect, you are prepared to evaluate and seek assistance, when appropriate, to bring your plans on track again.

Good retirement planning does not begin with money. It begins with recognizing our own behaviour (or lack of it) and how that can influence everything that follows in life.

It's MY Retirement

Jim Yih

When I think of retirement planning being personal, I think retirement can be anything you want it to be. When I ask people what they want to do when they retire, there are some responses that come about frequently like *"travel"*. When people think about what retirement looks like, visions of lying on a beach reading a book and drinking sangrias may come to mind. Or, maybe there are visions of golfing during a sunny blue-sky day with white sands and immaculate greens. This is what I call, *"retirement pornography"*. In other words, it is the kind of retirement that society says you should have to be successful. I think the roots for this type of thinking started out of one of the most successful advertising campaigns in the financial industry called 'Freedom 55'.

Retirement doesn't have to be sexy. In fact, most successful retirees will tell you retirement is about doing what you want to do. Although we may think we want to travel a lot in retirement, very few people can travel 365 days of the year or even 90 days of the year. Most traveling in retirement is limited to less than six weeks and the destination is not usually an exotic one.

Personal retirement planning is about figuring out what you really like to do with your time. It's about finding your passion and what makes you tick. It's about being motivated to get up every morning looking forward to what you've planned to do with your day.

For example, when I retire I may want to write more books, but instead of writing about retirement and finance, I may want to broaden my scope to write books about travel or for children. Some of you may look at that and say that's ridiculous.

The fact is, I don't care what you think because it's not your retirement. It's MY retirement and my retirement can be anything I want it to be.

Couples often use the language *"It's OUR retirement."* And although I think some retirement planning happens together, it is so important to start with the language that begins with *"my"* retirement. For couples to be truly happy in life, there has to be a balance between things you do together and the things you do alone. My wife loves to do crafts and scrap booking. Although that is something I'm not too interested in, she should find ways to build it into her retirement plan, if that is what makes her happy. For me, it might be golf. Once we take the time to discover ourselves and what makes each of us happy, we can then compare dreams and see where those dreams overlap. Never assume that you already know your spouse 'retired'. Instead, ask about his or her goals for retirement - you may be surprised at what your partner says.

You see, once you really understand the idea that retirement planning is personal, you will realize that it's all about finding yourself. Most people think retirement planning is all about money and how much is enough, but truly successful retirement planning is all about you and knowing who you are and what makes you happy.

Chasing the Goals of Others

Patricia French

People sometimes say they are struggling to find *"their own way"*. In practice, however, I am more likely to see people struggle to find *"other people's way"*.

This choice comes about when we look to others for direction. Why would you purchase a huge house if your heart rests in world travel? Is it because you saw it was important to your family, friends, and colleagues to buy the *"dream home"*, so you thought you had better get on board as well? As author and educator **Bernard Poduska** wrote:

> *"You can never get enough of what you don't need, because what you don't need can never satisfy you."*

Did your mom ever buy school clothes for you that were too big thinking you would eventually grow into them? My mom has always been an optimist. I never grew into those clothes before they wore out. Likewise, you will never grow into a financial plan that is based on the ideas of another person. Your plan has to fit you! Successful planning comes from understanding your goals and dreams and not trying to chase the goals and dreams of others.

In my professional work I see daily evidence of a concept called **locus of control**. People who demonstrate an <u>internal</u> locus of control accept responsibility for their actions, acknowledge mistakes, and are willing to seek support to correct them and move on. They feel in control of their behaviours, choices, and the resulting outcomes. At the other extreme, people who have an <u>external</u> locus of control believe that the world controls them and that they are like a dinghy at the mercy of a raging sea. For every negative outcome there is an excuse - it's the victim mentality.

"Excuses are the nails used to build a house of failure."
~ DON WILDER

Most of us fall between the two types, but lean to one type more than the other.

People who write and implement their own financial plan could be described as having an internal locus of control. As we get older, we tend to develop a stronger internal locus of control. This is likely because with maturity comes experience, expertise, and self-efficacy. Typically it is not until we're older that we feel ready or compelled to plan. Ultimately, a planner's success is a result of setting goals, becoming knowledgeable about options or strategies to reach those goals, and putting the plan into action, perhaps with professional assistance. I find many people *"shut down"* in the planning process before taking action. Is it fear that the plan may not work? Is it that the plan was made by an *"expert"* and doesn't fit? Is it that the plan will be a lot of work to get on the go? Remember that the plan should never be more important to anyone else than it is to you. It's your plan!

Taking action is by far the toughest step - it shows our commitment to the plan. Like that old adage says...when it comes to breakfast, the chicken is involved, but the pig is committed! When it comes to financial planning, the commitment must be our own!

Reference:

Poduska, B.E. (1993). *For Love and Money: A Guide to Finances and Relationships.* Brooks/Cole Publishing Company. Pacific Grove, California.

Exercise One

Making It Personal

The Retirement Card

I f someone asked you, *"What are you going to do when you retire?"*, what would your answer be? Does your reply show choices that would create a meaningful and productive retirement? The following exercise is intended to get you thinking, at a personal level, about how a retirement plan is created. In the space below, you'll see a box equal to the size of a business card. On the card, write the following:

~ **Your name** (centred - because the plan is about you - not someone else).

~ **One thing you would like to do "retired"** (write this below your name). Why one? Because you can't do everything at once. You have to begin with one.

~ **Where you hope to do this** (write this in the upper left hand corner). If you wrote "Travel", indicate in the top left hand corner which destination you are going to first.

TRIAL
TRAVEL #2
HEALTH

BILL DUNN
CAMP/HUNTER

Notes

2nd thing You Cannot Retire from Yourself

by

Rein Selles

MSc, PRP

I was teaching the retirement card exercise (see page 17) in Whitehorse, Yukon Territory, when an individual at the back of the room spoke up and said, *"I have one of those (cards)!"* I invited him to the front and he pulled a card out of his wallet that looked something like this:

Henry (Retired)
Toy Doctor
Repair and Refurbishing of
Well-loved Toys

Toys donated to the
Children's Cancer Unit

"This a wonderful retirement card!" I said as I looked at his name tag. *"But I'm confused. Your name tag says 'Tom' but the card says 'Henry'."*

Tom replied, *"Oh, some old guy gave this to me once and I liked it so much, I kept it!"*

I wondered then, *"How many people are walking around with someone else's plans for retirement in their minds or pockets?"*. There is another view of retirement that is very different. In the course of your travels you may have come across the following vanity plate that originated in Arizona:

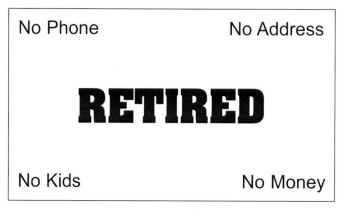

As you can see, there is nothing or 'no thing' associated with retirement. When placed as a license plate on a car as a form of grey humour among retirees, there is some truth in this joke. Some people would like the idea of retirement to go away.

WHAT IS RETIREMENT?

I have found it helpful, when teaching, to use the following definition:

> *"Retirement is a decision to terminate your current position in order to access pension income."*

In the past, pension plans in Canada required contributors to quit working before income from their pension plan could begin.

Age came into the definition of retirement because pension plans restricted payment until the contributor reached a certain age:

~ **Age 55** for most public and private pension plans in Canada excepting the federal Superannuation Pension Plan (as early as 50) and the pension plans of the military, RCMP and police forces.

~ **Age 60** is the earliest age for Canada Pension. Canada Pension Plan (CPP) will allow a reduced retirement benefit if Canadians apply between 60 and 64, but income from employment must be below the Canada Pension maximum income at age 65 for one month if working full-time and two months, without quitting, if earnings are under the maximum.

These rules all govern what we call <u>early retirement</u>.

Normal retirement in Canada occurs at the **age of 65**. There is, however, no requirement to stop working in order to receive Old Age Security payment. I term this a *"deemed"* retirement - a policy of the government of Canada that declares every citizen, regardless of employment status, to be retired and eligible for pension income based on residence, not employment, rules. Canada Pension Plan will also allow payment at 65 without ceasing employment.

If this all seems overly legalistic to you, then you have identified the problem. **Retirement is not the language of persons, it is the language of government (or the law)**. No wonder so many people cannot identify with retirement!

As part of my research, I noticed that specific groups of people in the population either chose not to use the word retirement in their planning or couldn't identify with the idea. They included:

Business, Fishing and Farm Operators
As one farmer said to me,

> *"Farmers don't retire - city people do that! If a farmer retires, he's six foot under. Then he is retired!"*

The same is true of many business owners. Why stop doing something you enjoy?

Professionals
While some professionals will retire early (by choice), most will continue in their careers well past *"normal"* retirement age. Included are doctors, lawyers, judges, architects, engineers, etc. The relationship to education and associated debt in this group should not be ignored. If one has spent six to 12 years in post-secondary education attaining the necessary qualifications for a career then, as a late starter, one would also not necessarily be interested in retiring early. The career would simply not have had enough time to develop. On the other hand, it is possible, for this group, that age related health changes become a more likely reason to retire than personal choice.

Homemakers
If you work full-time at home, there may not be any sense of 'retirement'. As one homemaker said to me,

"How will my life change at retirement? Everything still has to be done around the house! You don't stop living!"

REDEFINING RETIREMENT

If retirement is personal, then the definition cannot be based solely around work and pensions because you cannot retire from yourself. Try this definition instead:

"Retirement should be my 'preferred lifestyle'."

That opens up a whole new way of thinking and decision making.

For example:

"Why would I retire (stop doing what I am doing), if I can't see that my lifestyle would improve?"

Or as an alternate thought:

"Why would I keep working if my lifestyle in retirement is better than what I'm doing today, and I can get paid for doing it?"

Let me put this in the form of a conversation I had with a 68-year-old in a community in northeastern Alberta.

The gentleman came to me with this question,

"Do you think I should retire?"

"Why are you asking?" I said.

"My friends are telling me I should retire because of my age, but I got married late in life and my wife is younger and still working."

"Do you like your job?" I asked.

"I love what I do!" he said.

"Can you think of anything you would rather do?"

He said, *"There's nothing that I can think of."*

"Then as far as I'm concerned, you should keep working."

The pressure from others to make a decision to retire can include spouses, friends, relatives and colleagues. As the pressure to retire increases around a person, the fear and uncertainty about making the *"right"* decision also increases. After speaking to a teachers' group in southern Alberta, a 66-year-old teacher came to the stage in tears to thank me.

"What for?" I asked.

She said, *"You are the first person who has ever talked about retirement in a way that gives a person permission to work and not retire. I love my lifestyle and I don't want to change it even if I am over 65!"*

And she is absolutely right.

NOT RETIRING

To not retire at all is a choice that is occurring more frequently in the Canadian population as greater numbers of older adults make conscious and deliberate decisions to continue working regardless of age or pension eligibility. In addition to valuing a working lifestyle, other factors that may prompt a person to not retire can include:

~ **Economic considerations** that involve payment of debt and the need to replace capital lost in the raising and education of children, divorce or other reason. A sudden and unexpected change in the value of assets due to market volatility can change one's perception of the ability to retire.

~ **Family considerations** include delays brought about with late life marriages and the later birth of children. The potential conflict in goals between retirement and children generally means that retirement loses out!

~ **Multiple moves over a career** can significantly affect the degree of pension income or capital saved for retirement. I am meeting more people in classes today who are *"short service"* to their preferred retirement date and have chosen to continue working as a result.

~ **Employment market pressure** can influence people to keep working. The aging of the workforce means that organizations need and want their older workers to stay and are prepared to make work a more interesting prospect than retirement.

NEW RETIREMENT OPTIONS

Prior to 1991, most Canadians attributed their reason to retire to 'changing health'. Then, during the 1990's, 'the economy' became the predominant factor in the decision. It has only been in this decade that personal choice has really become possible. **Sherry Cooper** in her book, *The New Retirement,* attributes the new opportunities possible in retirement to the fact that the generation currently planning retirement (baby boomers) are more active in mind and body. It is certainly true that good health at retirement offers the most potential for establishing a preferred lifestyle. If you view the choices at retirement from the perspective of the outcomes, you would be faced with the following:

To Fully Retire

This is what many Canadians would term *"traditional retirement."* The outcome is that you maximize your options within your lifestyle. Work may be a part of retirement but only in the form of volunteer work. Income is drawn solely from pensions and assets that were saved for retirement.

To Retire But Return to Some Work

If I ask a group planning retirement today how many would prefer this choice over full retirement, nearly 80 to 90% will choose this option. Their goal is to, *"work for the fun of it."* The fact that the retiree gets paid for that work is just a bonus. For some, however, the money allows for activities and choices that might not otherwise be possible.

With the aging of Canada's workforce, governments have also been forced to rethink their definitions of retirement. As mentioned earlier, it was written in the law that an individual had to retire (quit work) in order to be eligible for pension benefits at a specific age. Laws governing pension plans, at the time, also restricted the pensioner's ability to return to work if that work involved the same employer. You may recognize the term *"double dipping"* associated with this issue.

Since 2000, however, federal and provincial governments have amended legislation to encourage greater retention of older workers and remove obstacles that would allow a return to work after retirement. In Alberta, the public service pension plans permit an employee to retire (take the pension) and return to work without restriction. The warning I give the employee, however, is that when you say, *"I quit"*, a group of people around you may also be saying, *"Oh good!"* You may not be welcome back after retirement.

To Keep Working

Choosing this option will produce the best outcome financially since income and benefits continue uninterrupted. The outcome of full-time work is that it maximizes your benefits while maintaining your present lifestyle.

To Reduce Your Workload (Balanced Lifestyle)

I like participants in my workshops to compare the option of retirement and a return to some work with the option of a reduced workload. The difference between the two is that benefits (prorated) continue even though income is lower. Here is how it would be presented:

> *"If you retire, take your pension, and then come back to work, you lose your benefits - including paid holidays! Instead of retiring, what if you could add an extra day to your weekend (work .8). Your income would decrease proportionately but your lifestyle would be more balanced. In effect, you get the opportunity to practice retirement before you actually quit."*

The Harris Poll in 2004 found that as many as one-third of those retired in the survey would have preferred to keep working if a reduced workload had been offered.

To Keep Working AND Collect Pension

The latest twist in retirement options came in December, 2007, when the federal government amended the Income Tax Act to allow contributors to pension plans, who attain an *"unreduced benefit"* under the terms of the pension plan, to take up to 60% of the earned benefit as pension income while continuing to contribute to the pension plan.

At first glance it doesn't seem to make a lot of sense. The issue for the government and employers is **retention**. For example, Sue is a nurse, who by the terms of her pension plan reaches the *"85"* factor (or 30 years of service and age 55) for an unreduced benefit and might initially think about retiring (taking the pension). She could then come back on a casual basis. But, what if Sue were able to earn full-time pay and benefits while collecting 60% of her pension? Even though her income tax might increase, she would still be taking home significantly more income. The opportunity for some Canadians to recover financially from raising a family, mismanaged personal finances, or a marital change can be a real incentive to keep working. The downside to this choice is the risk that health may change before retirement can become a reality.

RETIREMENT IN FAMILIES

There are many jokes about the danger of retiring *"together"* and like most humour, the jokes contain an element of truth. Too much togetherness can test relationships - even good ones. It is my belief that couples who do retire together may be more willing to communicate and may be more sensitive to each other's needs than those who have one family member retiring before the other. The terminology for the types of retirement within families are:

Synchronized Retirement
Representing those families who choose to time their retirements together.

Dissychronized Retirement
Representing those families with individuals who choose to retire before their partners. Most couples in Canada will likely follow this form of retirement due to differences in age at marriage. Since men tend to marry younger women, dissychronized retirements may be male first in many cases. Here are two key challenges in planning retirement together:

~ The individual who retires first is always at an advantage in that he or she can create his or her lifestyle of choice without accounting for those choices to another.

~ The pressure will always be greater for the one who retired first to accommodate (or make room for) the other person when he or she retires.

A female spouse in northern Canada spoke out at a workshop on this issue in the following way:

"I told my husband that he was going to work until he dropped dead! There is no way that man is going to sit at home and get in my way."

It was interesting to me that the spouse wasn't at the retirement planning workshop - he had been told to work that day!

SUMMARY
You are the sum of all of the skills, experiences, and knowledge you have gained by living to this point. None of that can be taken away by retiring. **You can quit working but you will still have to live with yourself.** So who are you? What do you want to be as you continue to grow up? We have nothing to fear from retirement, except ourselves. This is real, it is personal and it cannot be assigned to another.

Retirement -
Your Dream Job

Patricia French

To many younger people I work with, retirement seems to be a rather vague destination that's way down the road - something they can worry about later. They have not been planning for retirement because their focus is on the present. Unable to imagine a future when they wouldn't have to work, the endless list of today's needs and wants takes precedence over planning for their *"retirement years."*

Over the past 10 years, the average retirement age of Canadians has been hovering around 62, with public sector employees retiring earlier (age 59) than both their private sector (age 62) and self-employed (age 66) counterparts (Statistics Canada). Canadians also tend to return to work after *"retiring."* About half will be back to work within two years.

I am grateful to have been exposed to a different view of retirement in my 20's. More than a decade ago, while working with Rein, I attended his course, *"Planning for Personal Freedom."* It was unlike anything I had seen or read about retirement. Rather than money as the message, it was lifestyle. If you understand the lifestyle you plan to lead, you can determine the amount of money necessary to support it.

The *"retirement card exercise"* on page 17 is a key one about identity and lifestyle. Think about when you first meet someone. Right after your name, do you exchange information on what you do for a living, whether homemaker or business executive? These social interactions attest to our use of work labels or titles to define ourselves and others. Before retirement, work is a huge component of our identity. Could that be one of the reasons the transition to retirement can be such a struggle?

In retirement, not only do you change your *"title"*, you have to fill the time that was taken up by working. If you include the time at work, the time to travel to and from work, and the time to prepare for work, a full-timer could be looking to fill 50 hours a week or 2500 hours per year with activity. Trying to fill that with golf may be impossible!

While working, people need to plan and practice for retirement. Plan for the lifestyle you want and practice those things you want to do while retired. If you don't travel before retirement, it's unlikely you'll travel when retired. Have you heard the adage: past behaviour is the best predictor of future behaviour?

Who will you be once you retire? I believe you will be who you are now. If you have nothing else in your repertoire to define yourself with today besides work, you may question your identity in retirement. Continuing or returning to work is great, if that is what drives you. People work following retirement for many reasons, but some will prefer work, paid or volunteer, to maintain *"identity"* and work/life balance.

Since work is such a big part of the lifestyle we know today, perhaps it helps to approach retirement like your dream job. How would you write that job description?

Making Retirement the Best Years of Your Life

Jim Yih

I remember a discussion I had with one of my clients. She could not wait to retire because she hated her life. She thought that retirement would be her new start for the good life and she would then become a happier person.

I see retirement as an opportunity to do different things with your time. I caution people from thinking they will magically become a different person overnight just because they retire. In reality, when you retire, you will likely still be the same person with the same values, beliefs, experiences and habits you had before you retired. The person you are before you retire shapes the person you will be after you retire.

If you want retirement to be the best years of your life, then the time to start making it happen is today. Everything you do today shapes who you will be in the future. Just because you have a little more time does not necessarily mean you will have a happier life. It's all about what you do with that time.

It is also important to realize that success at work does not necessarily translate to success in retirement. As a financial advisor, I've had the pleasure of working with some very successful people. Often that success, at an individual level, came about through work. Maybe they made a lot of money, or they held an important position, or they built a successful business.

What is interesting is that sometimes successful people have a greater difficulty living a successful retirement. Our careers can define who we are as people. In most introductory conversations, the question *"What do you do for a living?"* usually comes up within the first three minutes.

There are those who have made and accumulated significant amounts of wealth, and financially, they have the means to retire. But having enough money is not enough for a successful retirement. True success comes in figuring out who you are and what makes you tick. What are the passions in your life? What do you love to do with your time? What is it about work that you will miss when you retire? When you have answers to some of these questions, then you will be heading on the right path to making retirement the best years of your life.

If we believe that retirement should be the best years of our lives, how many of us are already living the best years of our lives now? For me, retirement planning is simply an extension of life planning. We should always be trying to improve our lives by repeating the good and replacing the bad. We should always be trying new things to keep life from being stale. Don't wait till retirement to try these things. Start before retirement. I learned these words from Rein:

"Practice retirement a little more each and every day to help you make your retirement truly the best years of your life."

Making It Personal
Developing Your Work/Life Balance in Retirement

Use the form below to consider how to create your
preferred lifestyle in retirement.

What I Like About My Job	Can Be Replaced By
-/*INTERESTING* - *LOTS OF "MUST DO's"* - - *SATIFACTION OF REACHING* *GOALS* - *WORKING WITH OTHERS'* - *TEAM WORK*	- *PART TIME* - *VOLENTEER*

What I Dislike About My Job	Will Be Gone!
- *ALL CONSUMING - TIME* - *LITTLE FLEXIBLITY*	*MORE TIME* " *FL* —

Making It Personal
Refining Your Work/Life Balance in Retirement

If what you like about work cannot be replaced through your lifestyle in retirement, then the question becomes, how much work is needed for you to feel that you have achieved your *"preferred lifestyle"*? On the meter below and using the results of the exercise you just completed, indicate what percentage of work would achieve the balance.

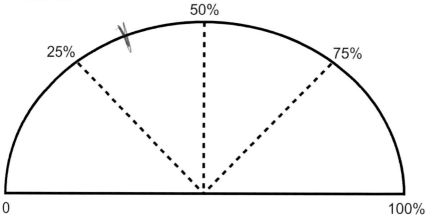

As the last step, check off the kind of work you would prefer doing. This will indicate the approach you will take to planning your own retirement.

_____ Doing the same work in the same organization

_____ Doing the same work in another organization

__✓_____ Doing the same work in another setting (this can include overseas opportunities such as teaching English as a second language)

_____ Using my existing knowledge and skills to create a small business or consulting venture

_____ Learning new skills and applying them in a new career

_____ Being a mentor and either coach or teach others to achieve results in my field

3rd thing Retirement is More about Spending than Saving

by

Rein Selles

MSc, PRP

RSP season in Canada runs from January through February each year and represents a period of advertising that is intended to encourage Canadians to save for retirement. In the months leading up to this period, banks and insurance companies will commission polls to test Canadian perceptions and behaviours around saving for retirement. Unless you lived in a log cabin deep in the woods, there is no escape from the message - *"YOU NEED TO SAVE."* Ironically, if you did live in that cabin in the woods, you probably wouldn't need to save!

How much do you think you need to save for retirement? Using the numbers below as representative of all savings needed (registered and non-registered assets) to fund retirement, which number best represents the amount you think you need in order to retire?

More than	$1,000,000	✓___
	$1,000,000	___
	$900,000	___
	$800,000	___
	$700,000	___
	$600,000	___
	$500,000	___
	$400,000	___
	$300,000	___
	$200,000	___
	$100,000	___
Less than	$100,000	___

When you picked the number did you include:

	Yes	No

1. The capital value of your pension plan
through work? *54,000* _____ _____

If you participate in a Defined Benefit Pension Plan, chances are you may not know either the value of the benefit you are earning or the capital necessary to fund the benefit (also called the commuted value). Try this rule of thumb: For each $100 of monthly pension you expect, you would need $18,000 of savings available at retirement to fund it.

126,000

2. The capital value representing the income
you would receive from Canada Pension
Plan at your retirement? ✓ _____

3. The capital value representing the income
you would receive from the Old Age
Security program at 65? *108,000* ✓ _____

The point I want to make about these three assets is that you have no control over any of the savings since contributions are required by law or, in the case of Old Age Security, given as a gift in recognition of residence in Canada.

1→3   ≤ 288,00

****

4. The equity in your current home? ✓ _____
$ 250,000

5. The value of other capital assets such as
farm, recreational property or income
property? *≥ RRSP TFSA INV. ACCOUN A 620,000 APR/16* ✓ _____

Every time you make a mortgage or loan payment that decreases your debt, or when the market increases the value of your property, you also save.

****

6. The estimated value of any estate that may
come to you in the future? _____ _____

7. The amount you plan to win in a lottery if
everything else fails! _____ _____

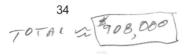

TOTAL ≈ $908,000

I include these last two because two polls in Canada in 2002 found that: 11% of those buying lottery tickets were doing so as a retirement plan (COMPAS), and 20% were waiting for an inheritance so they could retire (DECIMA).

WHAT IS THE PROBLEM WITH THE MESSAGE, "SAVE, SAVE, SAVE?"

In some respects Canadians need encouragement to save - particularly as the amount of personal debt increases. A survey by CGA-Canada found that a quarter of Canadians don't save any money at all, even for retirement. The accounting group indicated that Canadians are increasingly relying on borrowed money to finance day-to-day living expenses. (*Canadians In Debt Denial*: CGA's, CBC News posted on-line Thursday, October, 2007)

On the other hand, there are Canadians saving for retirement who, in reaction to the savings message, continue to accumulate wealth despite the fact that they may have *"enough."* As children of parents who were defined by the Depression Era, the possibility that there may *"never be enough"* can drive some Canadians to work long past their normal retirement age.

The message the financial industry is sending to Canadians is missing a level of balance. If you know that savings may be critical to income replacement, your knowledge of how you spend will help you understand the level of savings needed.

THE LIFESTYLE (SPENDING) APPROACH

Retirement, as a lifestyle, should be measured as more than one single period of time. While you may be retired for a period longer than your working life, your lifestyle will still change over that period. With longer life expectancies for the baby boomers, retirement may represent a period of 35 to 45 years. Unlike the retirements of our parents which were much shorter and characterized by at least one chronic health condition, baby boomers can expect a much more diverse lifestyle in their own retirements. It may be more effective to plan with three stages. The choice of a specific age range of 15 years for each stage is intended as a guideline rather than a fact.

Active Retirement (G.P -60)

Stage One is the period from retirement to 69. It is the time in our retirements when we can expect to be most **ACTIVE**. In fact, it is not very different from current mid-life (40 to 54) since anything is possible. It is not surprising then, that many of today's retirees see the value of continuing work in Stage One as part of their retirement lifestyle.

The language of Stage One can be heard in this statement,

"I'm so busy now, I can't find the time to do all the things I want to do."

Stable Retirement (GO SLOW)

Stage Two, STABLE retirement, often begins between 70 and 84. The term *"stable"* refers to the fact that many individuals at this stage develop lifestyles that reflect a pattern (e.g. shopping on Tuesdays, banking on Fridays, etc.). Much of the patterned behaviours can be attributed to a need to conserve energy to maintain activities of daily living. Having a routine requires the minimum of thought and yet allows the individual to enjoy life. For many, Stage Two can be the most enjoyable period of retirement and can continue through to one's death.

Limited Retirement (NO GO)

Stage Three, the last stage (85+) of retirement, occurs under two circumstances: loss of health and/or loss of financial security. In either case, the individual's lifestyle choices become LIMITED. In order to maintain one's lifestyle (i.e. living in one's own home), the individual may require some level of support. This support could come as formal support from government or agencies, or through informal means by family and friends. When this support is not available or too costly, lifestyle choices become limited.

By viewing retirement in these three stages, retirement planning becomes very interesting.

Financial Planning for Retirement

When are you likely to need the most income? Stage One since you will be doing the most! When are you likely to have the most disposable income? Stage Two, since the need for income decreases as lifestyles become simpler. There is a real fear that Stage Three may represent a period of higher spending given the need for assisted living or greater nursing care. Some planners will approach this as a legitimate risk that could be managed with a form of insurance that pays out a block of tax-free capital while you are alive called Long term care insurance. (See page 101)

Planning Your Housing

When would be the best time to move? Well, it depends. If your house is ready for retirement, the maintenance and repair cycle is not likely to begin for 10 or 15 years. So, perhaps the best bet is to move just before Stage Two while the energy is still there to handle the stress.

What kind of house would you look for? A Stage Three house, of course - one that allows you maximum independence (no stairs, wide hallways, large bathroom, lots of natural light, etc.). The worst time to move is in Stage Three since it represents a forced choice - no choice at all.

Relationships in Retirement

When are you likely to see the most people? Stage Two, because people seek out relationships in recognition of their own aging. If those close to you are lost by death, you quickly learn to value those who are still alive. In Stage One, you are too busy with your active lifestyle! When will you need people the most in your life? Stage Three when support is required.

The idea of *"staging"* plans is to give you a sense of how lifestyle and financial requirements might come together in a plan. At the same time planners will recognize that not everyone can be neatly assigned a label.

HOW WILL SPENDING CHANGE?

Given that lifestyles are likely to change, spending will change accordingly. While spending changes will differ individually there are general patterns that have emerged when comparing retirees to the rest of the population. Based on a Statistics Canada Review in 2005, Alberta Seniors and Community Supports reported a number of distinct differences in spending between seniors (over 65), the majority of whom are retired, and working families:

~ *Overall (average) spending by seniors ($40,956) represented 49.5% of expenditures of Albertans under 65 ($82,689).*

~ *Approximately 76% ($30,954) of senior households' average total expenditure went towards consumption expenditures compared to 70% ($57,691) for other Albertans. (Note: Consumption expenditures include: food, shelter, household operation, household furnishings and equipment, clothing, transportation, health care, personal care, recreation, reading materials and other printed matter, education, tobacco products and alcoholic beverages, games of chance, and miscellaneous expenditures.)*

~ *While seniors spent more on shelter (21%), those under 65 spent more on personal taxes (22%). Taxes only accounted for 14% of overall spending for seniors.*

37

~ Non-seniors spent more on home maintenance and repair ($488 on average) than seniors ($355) and such maintenance was reported less frequently by seniors (32%) than those under 65 (45%).

~ Despite all the stories regarding the cost of health care in retirement, seniors in 2005 spent an average of $1,733 per person, an amount $487 less per person than that spent by Albertans under 65.

~ Finally, while retirement may represent an opportunity to spend for the "fun" of it, the study reported that, "Seniors spent considerably less on recreation than Albertans under 65 in 2005. Seniors spent an average of $2,416 per person on recreation, compared to $5,658 for non-seniors."

PLANNING INCOME AND EXPENSES

The question, *"How much is enough?"* can best be answered by, *"What do you need?"* What you need may not be a single number. Consider the following:

Your Basic Lifestyle reflects an amount of spending needed over your lifespan (regardless of what stage you are in). The amount includes those areas that are critical to survival - food, shelter, utilities, insurance, health care, and transportation. No matter what lifestyle you lead over the course of retirement, this level of spending will rank first and will be your priority for planning.

A critical area within Basic spending is continuous drug coverage. If you are in a group supplementary health plan, review your options at retirement. The concern is that any existing medical condition that requires drug treatment may mean that your application for coverage can potentially be denied.

Other benefits gained through employment may also change:

~ Group life insurance may cease unless converted to a personal policy at cost. The option to convert group coverage to a personal policy, while guaranteed regardless of medical condition, could be very expensive so have a professional insurance broker compare options for you.

~ Disability insurance will end at retirement. Depending on age and whether you apply for CPP retirement benefits, your disability coverage through Canada Pension may still extend into retirement IF you plan to earn an income. At 65, eligibility for disablity insurance will end.

~ Vision/dental plans generally cease unless the employer offers a bridge benefit to age 65. Check with your optometrist and dentist as to the need for insurance in these areas. It certainly doesn't make sense to buy insurance when the premium is greater than your annual cost of service.

Primary Income

Your Basic spending should be matched by a form of income that represents sources which:

~ Pay through your lifetime; and,

~ Adjust with inflation (by law or by arrangement).

The income sources that best reflect these objectives are **pensions** from employment or those you create using capital (annuities), Canada Pension Plan and Old Age Security. Because it is your goal to always have this level of income, the objective will be to *"fix"* the payment. Hence the term *"fixed income"*.

Too much primary (or fixed) income can create other problems in later life. While the good part of fixed income is that the next cheque always arrives, the bad part is that the cheque always arrives - even when you haven't spent the last one!

Your Discretionary Lifestyle consists of those areas of spending over which you have a choice. They are most often associated with the quality of life and include travel, recreation, second vehicles or RVs, gifts, charitable giving, and some types of insurance. These expenses are most likely to change through the various stages of your retirement and may decrease with age.

Secondary Income

Because discretionary spending is <u>variable</u> through retirement, income design needs to be flexible and have two priorities:

~ It should be created in consideration of tax (as income increases, tax rates may also increase); and

~ You will need to be prepared to be personally involved in the decision making.

39

At some workshops participants will express concern as to how retirees cope with costs associated with changing health - particularly when confronted with the needs of aging and frail parents. Based on my experience, much of the adjustment in spending is done by reallocation of dollars from the Discretionary level to the Basic level. A participant reassured one of my workshop groups with the story of his father, a widower, who lived in an assisted living project in northern Alberta:

"My father pays $1,700 per month after tax to live in his facility and there is not one further cent he has to spend. All of his needs are taken care of and he is still banking the rest of his retirement income."

There will be situations that can create a tremendous drain on income and capital. Here are some hardships that I have witnessed with retired individuals and families:

~ A family that was supporting a child custody battle on behalf of their daughter. Almost all of their retirement capital had been devoted to this cause. Luckily they couldn't touch his pension plan, so they still had an income at retirement.

~ A family that supported the post-secondary education costs of all three of their children through graduate and post-graduate degrees. At retirement, while the couple had no retirement savings, there was tremendous pride in the achievements of their children.

~ A couple where one member of the family was confined to an Alzheimer's Unit while the other continued to maintain a personal residence and associated costs. The combination of double housing costs meant that there was little left over for any discretionary spending.

THE SAVINGS EQUATION

Should you save for retirement? Let's review the process you would use to make that decision:

1. You have determined your basic cost of living (in today's dollars) and measured your ability to pay those costs by the estimated pension income you will receive or can create at retirement, <u>after tax</u>. You know that this

income is assured for your lifetime and has the capacity to adjust either fully or partially with inflation.

2. You have begun to develop your interests in such a way that you can set priorities for spending that will make retirement fun. The amount of fun you will actually have will depend on these issues:

   a. Will you work in retirement? Earned income from employment, self-employment or revenue property can supplement income that is not yet available from pension plans due to early retirement. Note that the minute you work for pay, you may not need as much income from savings.

   b. The employment income that continues for your partner may make a significant difference in maintaining lifestyle without needing to access your retirement savings.

   c. Will you retire past the normal retirement age of 65? The irony of our retirement income system is that the older you are when you retire, the more potential primary income (pensions) you may be paid. In some two-pension income families, pension income may not only pay for the basics but may also cover all of your discretionary requirements. This can present a real problem for the withdrawal of savings from registered vehicles like RRSPs because of the potential tax that has to be paid on RRIF income earned after age 71. Test this with your own parents, if alive, to see if they ended up with **too much money** as they got older.

The need to save is directly related to the goal **to retire early**. The earlier the planned retirement, the more personal savings may be needed.

Can everyone retire? I believe so but not the way the media suggests. **Malcolm Hamilton**, the senior actuary for William Mercer, in an address to the Retirement Planning Association of Canada in Calgary in 2002 put the planning task in the following way:

"Life is filled with risk including:

   ~ *the stock market*

   ~ *your health*

41

- ~ *social programs*
- ~ *ax policies*
- ~ *inflation*
- ~ *interest rates*

*You can't manage these risks if you are determined to retire at a certain age, with a certain standard of living. **Live frugally, save what you can, retire when you can afford to, and manage to a budget thereafter.***"

So the key is to stay flexible. Be the tree that bends with the wind and you may live to retire at a ripe and rich old age.

The Budget - Blasphemy?

Patricia French

As a financial counsellor, I see value in making and using a budget. Certainly, some financial authorities denounce the idea by insisting few people budget well so why bother. I have reviewed and helped create budgets for countless clients and in the process have come to one significant conclusion - most of us do not know where our money goes. As a result, most of us do not know what we need. I believe that lack of financial self-awareness leads people one of two directions. Some worry about not having enough and save aggressively or work longer than necessary to appease their fears. Others blindly trust that when the time comes to retire, reductions in spending will occur to magically match their retirement incomes.

> *"He who does not economize will have to agonize."*
> ~ CONFUCIUS

Knowing what you spend now can give you a sense of how you will experience the transition to retirement. Earlier retirees are unlikely to experience an immediate dramatic decrease in spending. That may happen over time; but initially, work-related expenses may be the only substantial cost break.

Learning how you spend is an indispensable trick to help ease you smoothly into retirement. Tracking expenses is an omitted step in most financial plans. One reason that budgeting does not work for most people is they make a list of expenses based purely on their best *"guesstimate."* Sadly, we're poor guessers.

We also build a budget with only basics, like mortgage, utilities, and groceries, but overlook recreation/entertainment, repairs/maintenance of homes and vehicles, clothing, medical, and other irregular expenses.

43

If I only had a dollar for every time I've heard, *"I just don't understand why my budget is not working, my income is good"*. It's not about what we earn, it's what we keep.

You can create or perfect a spending plan with a little time and research. Three tactics will help you uncover your spending behaviour today, which will help you develop a budget that will work for you now and in retirement.

Strategy I: Watch Now
Track your expenses for two to three months and write down everything. This takes only seconds and a little honesty. Record every dollar that goes through your hands, including change for the parking meter or grabbing a coffee. The advantage is you'll see where your money is going as it happens. The disadvantage is, you're prone to experience accidental budget tightening caused by having to write it down. Not a negative outcome, but once you stop keeping track it's natural to drift back to your old habits. Total what you spend in each category and log it on your spending plan.

Strategy II: Look Back
Gather two or three months of bank, credit card and line of credit statements. This takes only an evening - a little time investment yielding thorough results. Most financial institutions make it easy to access statements on-line. With the exception of cash withdrawals, you will have a precise itemized list of everything you have spent. Every debit or credit card expense is identified by what, where, when, and how much. Group your expenses by category and input them on your spending plan. Don't forget bank service charges. The flaw of this method is the failure to track cash spending. Cash is easy to spend on the *little things*, like coffees and snacks, and you'll likely have no receipt to show for it. Add up the cash withdrawals and categorize them as your *"personal allowance."* Don't be surprised if cash spending really adds up.

> *"Beware of little expenses; a small leak will sink a great ship."* ~ BENJAMIN FRANKLIN

With either method, there will be a certain measure of guessing, because many expenses are sporadic, and may not have occurred during your reference period. Make safe estimates of those irregular expenses, like travel, clothing, and home and auto repair.

Seeing your spending on paper is as much about reducing spending on items you don't value as making room for expenditures you do value. Did you spend nothing on entertainment? If you would like to make it a priority, determine an amount and add the figure to your plan. Stunned by your bank service charges? Research if you have the right service plan. You can compare different plans on the website of the Financial Consumer Agency of Canada **(www.fcac.gc.ca)**. When you know what you've been spending, you can make more informed decisions going forward. Ask yourself if your current spending will be affordable on your retirement income?

Strategy III: Instant Gratification

Not convinced that making the effort to track will be meaningful? Then I propose a financial challenge to establish if you can afford your current lifestyle in retirement. Calculate the difference between your net working income and your anticipated net retirement income. As for the challenge... stockpile the difference between your pre- and post-retirement incomes in a separate account every month. If you need to dip into that stash, then you have more decisions ahead, and luckily time to do so. If you can consistently bank the difference, while maintaining your lifestyle, you can expect a stress-free transition to your retirement budget.

> *"My problem lies in reconciling my gross habits with my net income."* ~ ERROL FLYNN

Budgets work. Take the time to put your spending under the spotlight. Experience the satisfaction of deciding what you need and knowing you can make it work, now and in retirement.

How Do You Know How Much to Save, If You Don't Know How Much You Spend?

Jim Yih

While the message from the financial industry is the need to save more money, there are many cases where people are saving money blindly. In other words, they lose sight of why they are saving money in the first place.

SAVING FOR A RAINY DAY

My father at the age of 79 is still saving for a rainy day and quite frankly, I'm not sure that rainy day will ever come. My perspective on this behaviour is that sometimes retirees have a tough time spending their hard-earned savings because money provides security and nobody wants to run out of money. On the other hand, the message coming from the financial industry is one that creates the fear that if you are not careful, you may run out.

I recently sat down with a retiree who was frustrated by the recommendations of his financial advisor. Every time he wanted to take money out of the portfolio, the advisor convinced him to let it stay put, because spending the capital would enhance the risk of running out of money. Chances are this lack of spending will cause him to die with more money, result in more tax on the estate and generate a larger gift to his kids so they can spend it in ways he wouldn't approve of in the first place.

What was your original goal in saving? I would argue that the goal was for lifestyle. In other words, to use it in retirement to make retirement the best years of your life. So, instead of saving your money for a rainy day, why not use it for a sunny day when you can really enjoy it!

"YOU NEED $2,800,000 FOR RETIREMENT!"

A lot of people 'blindly save' because they are told to do so. This stems from financial calculators created by the financial industry - many of which are accessible on-line. These calculators can produce outcomes that may instruct people to save $2.8 million dollars for retirement. While that actual number may change, it is usually a number that is astronomically higher than expected. The size of the savings required may have more to do with the assumptions that went into the program than a person's real need. In other words, the output is only as good as the input.

Rather than saving blindly, try to gain a good understanding of all of the issues. This chapter outlines some important assumptions around saving that include non-traditional forms like employment pension, Canada Pension Plan and income from Old Age Security - all forms of income that last for your lifetime and may have provision to deal with inflation.

Instead of saving more money, maybe working longer is a good alternative. Labour force trends suggest that more and more people plan to work in retirement. At one time, if you worked after retirement you were considered a failure, because you did not save enough money. Today, work in retirement is not only perfectly acceptable, it is also becoming the norm.

When faced with a calculation that produces a large figure as a savings goal, check to see what assumptions for spending are being used. The financial services industry has a tendency to use rules of thumb. An example is the rule for income replacement. Advisors will use "70% of pre-retirement gross earnings" as a measure of how much income is enough to maintain lifestyle at retirement. My advice is to avoid rules of thumb wherever possible by knowing your spending today and how that might change in the future, at and during retirement.

MY TWO CENTS

The bottom line is you can't really understand saving until you've taken some time to understand spending. The root of financial success lies in your ability to understand how you spend money now (today) and how that spending might change in the future. I still remember the words of my dad (the consummate saver),

> "Always live within your means and you will never get in financial trouble."

Many people of his generation held this belief. In order to live within your means, you have to have some idea of your spending habits. With greater access to borrowing, it is very easy for adults to live beyond their means in the period leading up to retirement. There is a lesson to be learned from my father's generation. **Thomas Stanley**, author of the book the *"Millionaire Mind"*, believes one of the traits of wealthy people is their ability to understand their spending habits.

Exercise Four
Making It Personal
Calculating Basic Monthly Expenditures

The following expenses are most frequently associated with *"basic"* or survival lifestyle spending requirements. Note that where costs are annual, please divide by 12.

Food _____

Clothing (Replacement Cost) _____

Shelter _____

    Rent _____

    Condo Fees _____

    Utilities _____

    Repair/Maintenance _____

    Insurance _____

    Property Tax _____

Health Care Insurance (where paid) _____

Supplementary Health Insurance _____

    Co-insurance Costs (Drugs) _____

Vision/Dental _____

One Vehicle _____

    Insurance _____

    Gas & Maintenance _____

    License _____

Debt (Mortgage when planned into
retirement) _____

Other _____ _____

_____ _____

_____ _____

_____ _____

_____ _____

_____ _____

TOTAL BASIC _____

Exercise Five

Making It Personal

Calculating Discrectionary Monthly Expenditures

The following expenses are most frequently associated with *"discretionary"* or quality of life spending requirements. Note that where costs are annual, please divide by 12.

Travel	_____
Holidays	_____
Insurance (pick which you will use)	
Travel Insurance	_____
Life Insurance	_____
Critical Illness Insurance	_____
Long-Term Care Insurance	_____
Cable/Satellite TV	_____
High Speed Internet	_____
Cell Phones	_____
Clothing (Fashion)	_____
Furnishings (Redecorating)	_____
Household Incidentals (Newspapers, etc.)	_____
Entertainment	_____
Hobbies	_____
Second Vehicle and/or RV	
Insurance	_____
Gas & Maintenance	_____
License	_____
Gifts (Christmas, Celebrations, & Birthdays)	_____
Charitable Giving	_____
Season's Tickets	_____
Memberships	_____
Other _____	_____
_____	_____
_____	_____

TOTAL DISCRETIONARY   _____

The Best Retirement Plan is to Be Debt Free

4th thing

(or "I owe, I owe, it's off to work I go!")

by

Patricia French

MSc, PHEc

D ebt in retirement used to be a four-letter word. Times have changed and consumers are much more comfortable with debt - too comfortable. Debt can be a trap.

"Man is the only kind of varmint who sets his own trap, baits it, then steps in it." ~ **JOHN STEINBECK**

From my perspective, debt reduction must be the first priority of a financial plan. In the financial community, the goal of investing garners all the recognition and hoopla. Hundreds of books and websites purport to have investing figured out and each sells a surefire system from which the investor will reap great financial reward. Does paying down debt seem boring to you in comparison to investing?

Debt repayment is a sure thing. Where else can you find that every dollar *"invested"* gives you a tax-exempt, guaranteed rate of return equal to the interest rate on the debt? If you have a credit card at 18% with a balance, an extra dollar paid on that card will give you a guaranteed rate of return of 18%. Match that consistently with investments in the market!

Debt has become so normal that according to **Roger Sauvé**, in *The Current State of Canadian Family Finances 2007 Report*, it has risen seven times faster than the increase in household incomes, and the average household has over $80,000 in debt, up 22% since 2000. For many, monthly savings have been replaced by monthly debt payments. With rates of debt increasing, the percentage of people carrying their debt into retirement will also rise.

> *"The only reason a great many American families don't own an elephant is that they have never been offered an elephant for a dollar down and easy weekly payments."* ~
> MAD MAGAZINE

Can you expect your income to be lower in retirement? That is the norm. Could you manage your expenses, including debt payments, on less income - 30% to 50% less? According to a study by the **Certified General Accountants Association of Canada (CGAAC),** four in 10 adult Canadians feel their debt level hurts their ability to weather unexpected circumstances, and 28% of Canadians with debt see their debt as a significant barrier to realizing their retirement goals. Debt not only affects our sense of financial security today, it also weakens our likelihood of financial readiness for the future. It will pay to tackle debt by whatever means necessary, <u>now</u>.

HOW MUCH DEBT IS TOO MUCH?

While lenders will treat the amount of debt like a math problem, I believe that you will never lose by being debt free as you approach retirement. A key advantage is that you do not need the retirement or investment income to support the expense of credit card, loan or mortgage payments.

Lenders use two ratios to determine the amount of debt a borrower can manage: Gross Debt Service Ratio (GDSR) and Total Debt Service Ratio (TDSR). The word *"service"* refers to monthly payments - the amount of money needed to service (pay) certain expenses such as housing and consumer debt.

Gross Debt Service Ratio (GDSR) looks at the proportion of your income that is required to pay your basic housing costs. It includes the total cost of housing payments (principal, interest, taxes, and heating) divided by the family's total gross income. Your GDSR should not exceed 32%. Spending a greater portion of your gross income than 32% can make it difficult to cover other expenses. This can be called having a "housing burden".

Total Debt Service Ratio (TDSR) looks at the proportion of your gross income that is required to cover basic housing costs and all other consumer debts. It is the percentage of your gross monthly income that will be used for housing and other outstanding loans and debts. Lenders will usually allow up to a 40% TDSR, and it is rare to be able to borrow from a good lender, such as a bank, if your TDSR is above 40%.

Gross income is your income before deductions such as income taxes, Canada Pension Plan premiums, Employment Insurance premiums, and workplace benefits. For most borrowers, a TDSR of 40% would equal more than half of their take-home pay.

Keep in mind that the GDSR and TDSR are guidelines lenders rely on when extending credit. Consumers need to judge for themselves what amount of debt they can manage. Don't let your lender be the judge of what you can afford. Use your budget and your gut!

Look down the road - are there any factors that may impact how much debt you can afford? Are you planning to help out your kids, start your own business, reduce your work schedule or retire from work? Changes in lifestyle can reduce income and strain the budget. For example, if you are planning to retire in the next few years, borrowing should be limited to what you can afford on your retirement income. Many retirees are forced back into the workplace for financial reasons.

SPOTTING THE DANGER

"I'm living so far beyond my income that we may almost be said to be living apart." ~ **E.E. CUMMINGS**

In addition to your GDSR and TDSR, there are other ways to spot if your debt is starting to control your lifestyle. In the exercise below, check those statements that are true for you:

_____	Are you only able to make the minimum payments on your debts?
_____	Has your debt been increasing?
_____	Have you missed debt payments or had to take advantage of the miss-a-payment feature on your loans or mortgage?
_____	Have you used a cash withdrawal from one credit card or line of credit to pay another (also called kiting)?
_____	Are you at or near the limit on most of your credit cards?

_____	Have you obtained new credit because your current credit cards or lines of credit are at the limit?
_____	Have you borrowed additional money since consolidating your debts?
_____	Have you received a call from a lender looking for missed payments?
_____	Have you borrowed money from friends or family to make ends meet?
_____	Are you unable to set aside even a small amount of savings for a rainy day or emergency?
_____	Do you feel as though you are living from paycheque to paycheque?

If you checked more than a couple of questions, it's time to look at solutions and get some professional advice where appropriate.

DEBT MANAGEMENT SOLUTIONS

If you wish to reduce or, better yet, eliminate your debt before retirement, choosing the right strategy can save you time and interest charges. Managing debt can be tricky since there are many potential solutions. The solution best for you depends on:

~ **Amount of Debt** - Larger amounts of debt often require more aggressive solutions.

~ **Number of Debts** - Solutions that reduce the number of debts by consolidation may be beneficial.

~ **Strength of Credit** - With more established credit, solutions available through a lender, such as consolidation, may be options.

~ **Amount of Money Available to Pay Debt** - Finding money in the budget to pay down debts can make paying off debts faster and easier.

Increase Income and/or **Decrease Expenses** are appropriate solutions when the debt level is lower or when more money can be made available to pay debts. Work more or spend less to free up the money to add to your debt repayment. In retirement, this may mean getting back into the workforce. Not necessarily full-time, but enough to boost your income to pay off debt.

Refinancing refers to lengthening the duration of a loan in order to reduce the monthly payment. Good credit is essential for this to work, but extending the loan can help the payment fit better in your budget. If a loan will extend into your retirement, the trimmed-down payment will take less of your reduced retirement income.

Consolidation is often the preferred solution for reducing the total number of debt payments and reducing the overall interest. Good credit is vital and collateral is often required. This solution is especially effective if you have a number of debts or several credit cards with higher interest rates. One loan could pay them off entirely, trading several monthly payments for one loan payment at a better interest rate. Consolidation can be done with a loan or personal line of credit. Homeowners could also consider a home equity line of credit, a second mortgage, or rewriting the primary mortgage. Rewriting your primary mortgage can result in paying the consolidated debts over the lifetime of your mortgage, costing you piles of interest. This solution should be reserved for situations where your budget is so tight that you cannot afford to make all of your debt payments. (See Paying Off Debt with Debt - Making Consolidation Work.)

Negotiating with Creditors is helpful if you are experiencing a temporary financial setback. You can arrange with creditors to make reduced payments for a short period of time. This option may affect your credit, so attempt the previous options first.

Legislated and Non-Legislated Insolvency Programs are solutions of last resort. They include Debt Repayment Programs, the Orderly Payment of Debts Program, Consumer Proposal, and Bankruptcy. Debt can reach an unmanageable level and result in stress that's hard on individuals, couples and families. This can happen from taking on too much debt or from a change in circumstances, such as retirement. If your credit has been affected by an inconsistent payment history, you will be unable to take advantage of bank solutions. Legislated programs are available to assist consumers to recover from extreme financial problems and get back on track. Contact Credit Counselling Canada **(www.creditcounsellingcanada.ca)** to find a not-for-profit agency in your area that provides unbiased information about legislated and non-legislated programs.

IN YOUR BEST "INTEREST"

Borrowing can mean paying tens or hundreds of thousands of dollars in interest over a lifetime, much of it unnecessarily. So, if you have to finance, it's in your best *"interest"* to minimize your costs of borrowing. The first point to remember is that interest rates on loans, lines of credit, and mortgages are negotiable. Second, there are good on-line resources to help you shop around for the best credit value.

The Financial Consumer Agency of Canada **(www.fcac.gc.ca)** is an outstanding source of information on loans, mortgages, and credit cards. In particular, you can compare hundreds of credit card offers from different providers on a wide range of criteria including: minimum income required, minimum credit limit, interest rates (purchases, cash advances, and balance transfers), grace periods, minimum payments, annual fees, and rewards and benefits.

Just switching from a high interest rate credit card to a low interest rate credit card could save you 10% interest per year. If you are carrying a balance greater than $1,000, it makes good sense to switch to a low-rate card to help you pay the debt down faster. At a lower interest rate more of your payment goes to the principal. Even with an annual fee of $30 to $60, you will save money. You can switch back to the high-rate card after the debt is paid in full, and pay your card in full every month. If you pay the balance on your credit card in full every month, you don't need a low-rate card.

PAYING OFF DEBT WITH DEBT - MAKING CONSOLIDATION WORK

Taking out a new debt to pay off old debt won't work unless you understand the reason the debt accumulated. Make the necessary changes to prevent debt from accumulating again in the future. This may mean:

~ Tracking your spending so you understand where your hard-earned money is going,

~ Reducing spending so your money is going to things that you value and are consistent with your goals,

~ Monitoring your budget to stay on track and so you know what you can manage for a consolidation loan payment, and

~ Eliminating extra credit cards or lines of credit to help prevent accumulating new debt.

Before visiting your financial institution to apply for a consolidation loan, take the time to work out your budget. Knowing what you can afford for a consolidation loan payment will prevent you from taking on too much. It's natural to want to repay your debt as quickly as possible. If you try to be too aggressive your plan could backfire as you may find yourself short of money and using your credit cards again to cover the deficit. If necessary, take a longer borrowing term and make extra payments when you can.

MORTGAGES - A HOME IS WHERE THE DEBT IS

"People are living longer than ever before, a phenomenon undoubtedly made necessary by the 30-year mortgage."
~ DOUG LARSON

Since a home is the largest purchase most of us make, the mortgage will be our largest debt. Most consumers underestimate the amount of interest we will ultimately pay for home ownership. How do you make the right mortgage choice? Ask lots of questions of your lender and do your research. Mortgages can be complicated products and there are a myriad of alternatives on the market. The Financial Consumer Agency of Canada **(www.fcac.gc.ca)** and Canada Mortgage and Housing Corporation **(CMHC, www.cmhc-schl.gc.ca)** help to demystify mortgage options.

PAYING DOWN YOUR MORTGAGE FASTER

Paying off your mortgage early is a financial goal for many consumers. In Canada, we are inundated with *"expert"* opinions suggesting we should not rush to pay off our home. Unfortunately, much of this information comes from the United States, where interest on a mortgage is tax deductible. Since that is not the case in Canada, does it make sense to pay your mortgage off early?

The decision to pay extra on your mortgage should be evaluated within the context of your overall financial plan. For example, if you still have consumer debt, which is higher interest than your mortgage, pay it first. If making extra mortgage payments means you are unable to save for emergencies, save first.

Is there magic to paying your mortgage off faster? The trick is…**PAY MORE**. Extra payments are applied to your principal. Remember, early in your mortgage you are paying more to interest than you are to the principal. Extra payments can really shorten your amortization.

Shorten Your Amortization: When buying a house or renewing your mortgage choose the shortest amortization you can afford, while still meeting your other financial goals (e.g., saving).

Score a Lower-Interest Renewal: If the going mortgage rates are lower at the time of your mortgage renewal, or if you negotiate a cheaper rate than you had, keep your mortgage payment the same. Each payment will apply a few extra dollars to your principal, paying down your mortgage faster.

Make Prepayments: Ask your lender about prepayment options - extra payments you can make without being charged a penalty. They may include: doubling your payment (occasionally or regularly), boosting your normal mortgage payment by a prescribed percentage (e.g., mortgage payment +10%), and paying a lump sum on the anniversary of your mortgage each year up to a fixed percentage of the original mortgage. At renewal you can also put down as large a chunk on your mortgage as you want, without penalty. Squirrel away extra cash, income tax refunds, and work bonuses and drop it on your mortgage.

Accelerate Your Mortgage: You have likely heard that paying your mortgage more frequently will pay your mortgage off faster and save interest. Lenders offer semi-monthly, bi-weekly or weekly payments that make your mortgage more manageable budget-wise, but will only save you a few dollars. The big savings comes with choosing accelerated payment options. When compared to regular bi-weekly and weekly payments, accelerated bi-weekly and accelerated weekly payments result in an extra month's worth of payments per year and can save you a bundle.

Save-and-Pay Combo: Should you save in your RRSP or pay down your mortgage? How about both? Make contributions to an RRSP (personal or spousal), claim the contributions on your income tax, and then use the income tax refund as a lump-sum payment on your mortgage each year. Paying down your mortgage while investing in RRSPs allows you to meet two significant financial goals:

~ Getting rid of your mortgage as quickly and efficiently as possible to retire debt free.

~ Putting money early and consistently into RRSPs to maximize long-term growth to retire with financial security.

How much can you save? Consider a homeowner in the 32% marginal tax bracket with a $300,000 mortgage at 6% interest. If she saves $250 per month in an RRSP, the income tax refund based on her contributions of $3,000 per year would be $960. If she uses the refund each year as a prepayment, it would reduce her 25-year amortization by two years and save $26,000 in interest. As her income rises, she may be able to make higher RRSP contributions and pay her mortgage off even faster. Imagine a couple both using the save-and-pay combo!

COSIGNING

Our desire to rally around our families is powerful. Today's young adults are hanging around the nest much longer than previous generations. It is increasingly common to reach retirement with adult children living at home. Parents may not plan to have their adult children, or for that matter their grandchildren, living with them when they enter retirement. According to **Warren Clark's** report entitled *Delayed Transitions of Young Adults* based on the 2001 Census, four in 10 adult children between 18 and 24 and three in 10 adult children between 25 and 34 are still living at home with their parents. Some will have launched but boomerang back home to regroup after a relationship breakdown, job loss, or financial crisis. While adult children are often welcome, it can be an unexpected drain on your resources near retirement.

With high housing prices, and adult children spending longer in school and starting careers later, parents may feel compelled to help their kids make the challenging transition from the nest. Parents often have the wish to help their children get started purchasing property, buying a vehicle, or building credit. More than a cash injection, parents may offer or be asked to be a cosigner on a loan or mortgage.

Cosigning is risky! By accepting the responsibility, you assume a risk that a lender will not touch. That should be your first red flag. Though not intending to burst a supportive parent's bubble, the statistics are discouraging, with the Federal Trade Commission (FTC) finding 75% of cosigners having to pay when the borrower cannot. That can place an enormous amount of financial pressure on you at a very critical time.

If you are considering being a cosigner, remember the following:

~ You do not just help the borrower qualify; you are guaranteeing you will repay the debt in full in the event the borrower cannot. Could you afford to pay the debt in full or make the required payments on your retirement income? If your cash flow is inadequate to maintain the contract, then your personal credit will be negatively affected.

~ You may also need to pledge your own assets, such as your home, as collateral. Are you willing to risk your property in addition to your cash flow?

~ Any debt for which you cosign will be calculated into your GDSR and/or TDSR and will impact your own future borrowing ability. Cosigning could limit your ability to get a loan, or even a reverse mortgage yourself.

~ Cosigning may not be the best way to help your adult children build credit. Cosigned debts do not always appear on both the borrower's and cosigner's credit reports. Further, there are very good products on the market to help new borrowers build their credit within a year or two, without mom or dad.

Help if you can, but keep a sharp eye on protecting your own financial stability. Your children have time to get on their feet; do not let helping your kids knock you off yours.

SINGLES, COUPLES AND CREDIT

Whether living single or as a couple, you need to protect your credit for retirement. The best advice approaching retirement is to be debt free. This does not mean credit-free. This means actively using credit that is held in your own name. There are only two steps to protect your ability to borrow: have credit in your name and use it.

As singles, we begin to build our credit starting quite soon after high school. When we get into long-term relationships we merge our financial lives, including our credit by taking on debt jointly, from credit cards to mortgages. This has risks.

When fixed-term debts like personal loans and leases end, the associated credit report entry for the debt will show it as closed. Depending on the province in which you live and the credit reporting agency, the information about that debt will stay on your report for six or seven years. After that, the purge guidelines will drop the information from your credit report. Over time then, you will have fewer and fewer items listed on your credit report, and your credit may weaken due to lack of use. This is where revolving credit such as credit cards and lines of credit can be useful for protecting your credit. By continuing to use revolving credit and paying it in full each month, you will maintain your credit.

Debts held jointly as a couple should be reported on both partners' credit reports by the lender. Sometimes, however, only the person listed first on the credit agreement will have the debt and subsequent payment history documented on his/her credit report. The consequence for the second person on the agreement is that the good payment history may not be recorded and then will not be reflected in his/her credit score. Credit has to be used to be maintained - use it or lose it.

It is imperative that each partner continues to have and use credit that is in his/her name alone to maintain his/her personal credit identity. Though not nice to imagine, relationships end through separation, divorce, and death. To be on your own again, without good personal credit, can make starting over enormously challenging. Renting an apartment, getting insurance, financing a vehicle, or securing a mortgage or reverse mortgage may be out of reach.

The best practice for men and women is to maintain the credit you have, because it is much easier than rebuilding. Beyond investing, your credit is one more thing you want to save for your retirement. You never know when you might need it.

LOOKING AHEAD - PLANNING LONG-TERM BORROWING NEEDS

When you are working, your ability to borrow hinges on your employment or self-employment income. In retirement, borrowing ability is based on guaranteed forms of income. Lenders consider fixed types of income when extending credit, including work pensions, Canada Pension Plan benefits, Old Age Security, and annuity income. Retirement incomes drawn from investments such as RRSPs, RRIFs, or non-registered investments are neither fixed nor guaranteed, so most lenders exclude them from your income calculation. While you do not want to borrow more than you can afford to pay in retirement, it is easier to establish your access to financing, such as a line of credit, before you retire from work.

If you will carry your mortgage or other debt into retirement, then before leaving work, critically analyze whether you can manage your expenses on your retirement income. If it will be tight, discuss with your lender ways to bring your debt in line with your anticipated retirement income. Wait too long and qualifying may be much more complicated.

TAPPING THE MONEY TREE - GETTING MONEY FROM YOUR HOME

Time and time again the advice passed to the next generation and in water cooler discourse is that a home is the best investment you will ever make. Buying property is great advice, but the weakness comes from it being the only investment many people make. It foretells a dependence on your home for income. No doubt you have heard that it is not wise to put all your eggs in one basket.

There is more than one way to take advantage of the value of your home. Debt by choice is one option. This is, borrowing against the value of your home to augment income, renovate, travel, or give financial help to adult children or grandchildren. The common refrain of the house poor - *"I've got equity but no cash to spend",* has been answered by the lending community with options to tap your house for funds.

The CGAAC reports about one-third of Canadians who are still working see their home equity as an income source in retirement. There are uncertainties about home equity. You cannot predict the future value of your home at and through your retirement. You cannot be certain as to how long you and your spouse will want or be able to stay in your home. You cannot forecast the amount of income you can pull from your home because it is highly dependent on the housing market in your area, lending criteria, interest rates, household income, and personal credit. Finally, you do not know how long your retirement will be and how long your spouse will accompany you. Formulating your retirement plan assuming you will be able to get what you need from your house is precarious at best.

There are a number of borrowing options available to help you get money from your property: reverse mortgages, reverse mortgage lines of credit, conventional mortgages, and home equity lines of credit. Reverse mortgages and reverse mortgage lines of credit provide funds with no requirement for payments. Conventional mortgages and home equity lines of credit provide funds and at a lower cost, but the borrower's cash flow (income and expenditures) must be strong enough to manage the required monthly payments.

Reverse Mortgages (AKA Equity Conversion)

Reverse mortgages are a means for homeowners to access a portion of the stored value of their home to use today, while still retaining ownership of their home. In effect, converting the equity to cash.

Reverse mortgages are marketed very effectively. The portrayal seems undeniably convincing. Stay in your home. Remain independent. Maintain your financial freedom. Enjoy your money now; you deserve it. Renovate your house. Give your family money. Your home will continue to appreciate in value and offset interest costs and loss of equity.

Advantages: Reverse mortgages do not have to be repaid until you sell your home or you and your surviving partner pass away. The freedom not to make monthly payments can be a benefit for stretched budgets. You can repay the loan at any time. If the investment market has taken a downturn, a reverse mortgage could fill the gap until your investments stabilize or reach maturity. The amount you owe can never exceed the value of your property. High interest rates coupled with slow growth or decline in your home value make exhausting your equity a possibility; though, you and your beneficiaries will not be responsible for the shortfall. Depending on the provider, funds can be received as a lump sum, regular payments or a combination of a lump sum and regular payments. Lump sums may be the best choice for a project, vacation, gifting money, or investment. Creating a steady stream of income through regular payments fits when cash flow is the issue. The money received from the house is not considered income, so it will not impact income-tested benefits such as Old Age Security or Guaranteed Income Supplement. Interest paid on the reverse mortgage is tax deductible if the proceeds were used to earn investment income (interest or dividends).

Disadvantages: While your home may continue to appreciate in value and offset some of the interest costs and loss of equity, interest will rapidly accumulate on the amount you borrow. Historically, based on data from TD Bank, growth in Canadian resale home prices over the past 25 years has averaged 1.9% annually after adjusting for inflation, not the double digit growth seen recently. Using history as a guide, your rate to borrow could be four times your rate of appreciation. Due to start-up fees and higher rates of interest, reverse mortgages are more costly than conventional lines of credit or mortgages. Early payment of all or a portion of the amount borrowed could subject you to prepayment penalties. Borrowing against your home will impact the amount available to pass on to your beneficiaries.

Providers: Only two companies in Canada offer reverse mortgages: Canadian Home Income Plan (CHIP) and Seniors Money Canada. Mortgage brokers or Accredited Mortgage Professionals (AMP) will provide information and advice regarding reverse mortgage products. Reverse mortgage providers partner with banks, credit unions, mortgage brokers, financial and investment advisors, and other financial professionals who are then compensated for providing client referrals.

Reverse mortgages can be an expensive way to access some of the value built up in your home. Start-up fees can be significant and interest rates on reverse mortgages are much higher than standard mortgage rates. Start-up fees depend on options selected but typically include an application/documentation fee, home appraisal fee, and costs for independent legal advice. Fees can easily reach $2,000 to $2,500, which is deducted from the principal received.

In contrast to a standard mortgage, a reverse mortgage is a growing debt that consumes the equity in your home. Though the balance, principal borrowed plus accumulated interest, does not need to be repaid until you sell or pass away, it is quietly mounting and can reach a level that your remaining equity is too depleted to allow you to consider alternative types of housing, i.e., downsizing. You can run down your equity far faster than you built it. Both providers in Canada expect you to seek and pay for independent legal advice, to ensure you are entering into the agreement freely, that is, without pressure, and that you understand the contract and any potential risks.

Borrowing Minimums and Maximums: The borrowing limits vary between providers and are generally based on a percentage of the value of your home. However, the amount you can borrow through a reverse mortgage varies dramatically based on geographic location, the type of housing you own, your age and gender, and the amount of your current debt.

~ **Geographic Location:** Reverse mortgages are not available in every city, town, and village in Canada. People in smaller communities may not be able to access reverse mortgages at all. Also, homeowners in major urban centres are able to borrow a higher percentage of the value of their homes, due to the perceived stability of the housing market. If local market conditions change, reverse mortgage providers will tweak their lending criteria.

~ **Type of Housing:** Owners of single family detached homes can borrow a greater percentage of their home's value than owners of any other type of housing, i.e., semi-detached, townhouse, rowhouse, duplex, townhouse condominiums, apartment condominiums, and mobile homes (lowest percentage).

~ **Age and Gender:** The amount you can borrow, as a percentage of your property's value, increases as you get older. Minimum qualifying age requires at least one of the homeowners to be 60 years of age or older. For example, a 60-year-old is likely to be able to access around 15% of the value whereas a 90-year-old could borrow as much as 45%, depending on the provider. Ladies, you are expected to live longer, so you can borrow less of your home's value. The same rule applies to couples, because the amount you can borrow is based on the person with the greatest life expectancy.

~ **Amount of Current Debt:** While you can get a reverse mortgage even if you still have a mortgage, line of credit, or other personal debt, the amount you can borrow is reduced by your current debt. You must pay off any outstanding debt that is secured by your home with the proceeds, such as mortgages and home equity lines of credit.

Reverse Mortgage Lines of Credit

Reverse mortgage lines of credit are available at some credit unions in British Columbia and Ontario. A reverse mortgage line of credit functions like a reverse mortgage in that no payments are required until you sell your house, or you and your surviving spouse pass away. You may make payments of interest or interest and principal if you wish. The limit on the line of credit is based on similar criteria to the reverse mortgage: age, gender, property value, geographic location, type of housing, and amount of current debt.

Conventional Mortgages

If you have room in your budget to make payments and need a significant lump sum, consider a conventional mortgage rather than a reverse mortgage. Interest rates are much lower than those for reverse mortgages and are renegotiable should interest rates decline. You are not limited in the amount you can borrow by age, gender, geographic location, or type of housing, nor are you subject to the same borrowing limits. The lender will likely require a home appraisal. Your qualification rests on having the cash flow to support the payments.

Home Equity Lines of Credit

If your budget allows, a line of credit can be an effective way to tap into your home's value. Secured by your house, you can apply for a line of credit limited by the value of your home and your ability to make payments. This could be taken as a lump sum or used to regularly supplement income. Interest rates hover around the bank's prime lending rate making them economical. Start-up costs may include a home appraisal depending on the credit limit. Most have no annual fees and monthly payments range from interest only to around 2% of the outstanding balance each month.

These products are complex and all costs, advantages, and disadvantages should be carefully contemplated within the context of your overall financial plan. Before considering borrowing, consider the following alternatives to financing.

Downsizing

Consider downsizing by selling your home today and buying something less expensive. Downsizing today can give you the financial benefit of cash now without the downside of the financing costs (interest and fees). You will still own property and profit from appreciation in the housing market. This can also work if you still have a mortgage and downsize to a property you can purchase using the equity of your current home. Losing the expense of your mortgage payment is as valuable as an increase in your income.

Return to the Rental Market

Consider selling your home, and using the proceeds to supplement your income and renting accommodation. While there is uncertainty in the future of rental rates, so is there uncertainty in the future cost of utilities, property taxes, and home maintenance and repair. Estimate that your home will require 1% of its value each year for maintenance and repair. If this is not in your budget, your home could become a financial burden. If you decide to rent, paying the rent would be your only worry; maintenance and repair would be your landlord's problem.

Debt affects our financial security and can be a significant barrier to retirement. While the lending community has made borrowing in retirement appear simple and stress-free, nothing can compare to the ease of a debt-free retirement.

REFERENCES

Canada Mortgage and Housing Corporation (CMHC). (2008). *Reverse Mortgages*. Retrieved October 5, 2008 from:

    http://www.cmhc-schl.gc.ca/en/inpr/afhoce/tore/afhoid/fite/remo/

Certified General Accountants Association of Canada (CGAAC). (2007). *Where does the money go?: The increasing reliance on household debt in Canada*. Retrieved October 5, 2008 from:

    http://www.cga-canada.org/en-ca/ResearchReports/ca_rep_2007-10_ debt-consumption.pdf

Clark, W. (2007). Delayed transitions of young adults. *Canadian Social Trends*, 84, 14-22.

Federal Trade Commission. (1997). FTC facts for consumers: *"Cosigning a Loan"*. Retrieved October 2, 2008 from:

    http://www.ftc.gov/bcp/edu/pubs/consumer/credit/cre06.pdf

Sauvé, R. (2008). The current state of Canadian family finances: 2007 report. Ottawa: *The Vanier Institute of the Family*. Retrieved September 22, 2008 from:

    http://www.vifamily.ca/library/cft/state07.pdf

TD Bank Financial Group. (2006, September 14). Long-term outlook for Canadian home prices. *TD Economics Special Report*. Retrieved October 5, 2008 from:

    http://www.td.com/economics/special/ca0906_home_prices.pdf

When Debt Can Make the Heart Grow Fonder

Rein Selles

A few years ago I was teaching a group the basics of setting personal goals, and following a discussion on the merits of debt reduction, the group agreed that paying off debt was a great retirement strategy. That is - all but one person. She challenged the group and presented this alternate point of view.

> *"While I have always believed that you should be debt free, my father gave me an opportunity to be in debt that I couldn't pass up! My dad is a farmer and as part of the process of arranging the transfer of the farm to my brother, he purchased life insurance so that the rest of his children would be treated fairly at his death.*

> *"What surprised me was that he called me and invited me to buy additional insurance on his life as part of the original policy."* I said, *"Dad why would I do that?"* He said, *"What difference does it make who pays for the insurance? Think of it as a long-term investment!"*

> *"I told him that I didn't have any extra money and he encouraged me to borrow the money. And I did."*

The idea prompted more discussion and some humour as everyone wondered aloud if they could convince their own parents to try this unique form of family borrowing.

REVERSE MORTGAGING WITH FAMILY

When the question of reverse mortgaging one's principal residence comes up in class, I like to suggest an alternative strategy that involves family instead of private enterprise. The original case involved a retired couple and their three adult children.

Fulfilling a lifelong dream, the parents purchased a lot in their community, and with financing built their own home. As retirement approached, however, there was still some amount of debt remaining and the payments would erode their ability to maintain their lifestyle. I was asked to come and evaluate their options.

When I suggested that the couple could sell the home, pay off the debt and move into a smaller residence or rent, the reply was immediate,

"Oh we couldn't do that, we love this house and so do our children."

I asked, *"Have your children expressed interest in the house?"*

"Oh yes," she replied. *"My son is a realtor and if we ever had to move, he'd be the first to buy it."*

That got me thinking - what if the children could act as the couple's bankers?

"Your goal is to remain in this home as long as possible, but at the same time, you face the problem of servicing your debt with limited retirement income. Is it your goal that the children should have the house at your death?" I asked.

"That is what we hope will happen," he said.

I suggested, *"What if we invited the children to participate in the ownership of the house with you? By dividing the debt equally, none of the children are placed in a difficult financial position, and at the same time you can eliminate your payments. Since it is your intent that they should have the home anyway, this is their "stake" in the process."*

Both stories show how debt was used to support and build family relationships that are already strong. Mutual support between generations can sometimes fulfill retirement plans where traditional financial tools and products fail.

Is Debt Used for Investing a Good Form of Debt?
Jim Yih

As Patricia illustrated, debt is a huge part of our culture. We borrow to buy appreciating assets (like homes), depreciating assets (like cars) and even assets that have no marketable value (like consumer goods). Most Canadians borrow money to spend on things that are not financially productive.

One of the contributing factors to the debt crisis is the increased amount of leverage lending that has occurred. Leverage is a concept popularized by the financial industry and comes in many different forms. The basic root of the concept involves using borrowed money (someone else's money) to try to make money. By definition, leverage is any process that compounds risk because you could lose money that is not yours. Leveraging has been promoted as one form of good debt because it can be productive when it is understood and used properly.

Leveraging can magnify your return both on the upside and the downside. Let's assume you had $10,000 to invest and you were able to earn 10% growth in a portfolio of mutual funds. On the basis that the growth is capital gains, your return after you paid tax would be about 8.05% (assuming a 39% marginal tax rate).

Alternatively if you took the $10,000 and borrowed an additional $10,000 to make a total investment of $20,000, the return would increase to 11.5% after paying taxes and accounting for interest payments. That's a 43% incremental return. Leveraging is a way to supersize your returns so you can build wealth much faster.

When used properly, leveraging can be a productive tool to build wealth. At the same time, leverage comes with a caution because it can also be counterproductive without a proper understanding of the risks.

RISKS OF LEVERAGE

1. **Investment Risk** - Leveraging only works if you invest in investments that seek higher returns. Unfortunately that also means taking more risk that the capital values could change. Investment risk should be of primary concern to the investor because there are no guarantees for performance of the investment. Most leverage proposals illustrate higher returns but what if those returns don't come about? Because markets are cyclical, investors are pretty much guaranteed to have their share of losses as well as gains. When requesting a projection, make sure the advisor uses many different rates of return including scenarios where you lose money. Leveraging does not prevent you from making a bad investment decision

2. **Magnification of Losses** - Leveraging can boost your effective returns in good times, but it can also magnify your losses in bad times. For example, assume you invested $10,000, and then markets dropped and you were facing a loss of 10%. If you needed access to the money and sold (triggering your loss), your return after you paid tax would be about -8.05%. If you took the $10,000 and borrowed an additional $10,000 (at 7.5%) to make a total investment of $20,000, the loss would be magnified to -20.7% after paying taxes and accounting for interest payments. In real dollars, this means your $10,000 has lost $2,067.50.

3. **Interest Rate Risk** - There are a number of variables that affect your total return including tax, investment return, and the cost of borrowing. The key to successful leveraging is to have your after-tax investment return exceed your after-tax cost of interest. Therefore, rising interest rates can potentially have a negative effect on your leverage returns.

4. **Cash Flow Risk** - Rising interest rates have a ripple effect on your cash flow since payments increase. Prudent leveraging will ensure that you budget for the potential of higher interest rate costs and the subsequent effect on cash flow.

5. **Margin Call Risk** - One of the most annoying risks of leveraging is the dreaded margin call. The margin is the difference between your investment portfolio value and the amount of the loan. If the

market value of your investment drops and falls below a certain margin, the lender can issue a margin call where you will have to put in more money to make up the difference. Margin calls always seem to happen at the worst possible time. To help minimize the risk of a margin call, you can secure the loan with an asset like your home. Otherwise it is imperative that you only leverage within your financial comfort zone. Always budget a cushion in case you must respond to a margin call. Some institutions now have leverage programs that guarantee no margin calls.

6. **Emotional Risk** - Investing with or without leverage has its ups and downs. What is important is that leveraging magnifies the emotional rollercoaster. You will love the ups way more but the downturns can be incredibly painful. Are you in a position, emotionally and financially, to weather these ups and downs? Being able to sleep at night is key with leveraging because there are so many variables that can affect the success of a leverage plan. If you are at all uncomfortable emotionally with making interest payments, facing loss or having to deal with any of these risks, think twice before borrowing to invest.

Make sure you understand both sides of the leverage. There's no question that leveraging has the potential to make money if markets go up and interest rates stay low. However, markets don't always go up and interest rates could climb. If someone pitches leveraging to you, make sure both the rewards and the risks are presented. My observation of client experiences with leveraging includes far too many cases where leverage did not result in the best-case scenario.

MY TWO CENTS
Personally, I am not against the concept of borrowing to invest. However, I think leverage, as we call it, is over-promoted and oversold. It is time to change the way we think about debt. Instead of going into more debt - even if it is good debt - we should start focusing on paying down our other debts first. Ironically, it is those people who are more financially secure who can handle the risk of leverage but probably don't need to take the added risks. When it comes to leverage, I believe in one simple thing: make sure you are educated.

Exercise Six

Making It Personal

Targeting Debt - Do It Yourself (DIY)

To position yourself to efficiently pay off debt, you should work out a step-wise plan. Begin by completing the following table with your current monthly debt obligations. This will help you gain a realistic perspective on your current debt. You will clearly see your debts, the amount of credit you have available to you, what it costs you each month to service the debts, and the rate of interest you are being charged each year.

List your debts from highest annual percentage rate of interest (APR) to lowest interest. If two of your debts have the same interest rate, list the one with the smaller balance first. The order will ordinarily be: 1) Retail Credit Cards, 2) Bank Credit Cards, 3) Consumer Loans, 4) Personal Lines of Credit, 5) Home Equity Lines of Credit, and 6) Mortgages.

Debt	Annual Percentage Rate of Interest (APR)	Credit Limit (If Applicable)	Current Balance	Required Monthly Payment
	TOTAL			

Here's an example of a completed table:

Debt	Annual Percentage Rate of Interest (APR)	Credit Limit (If Applicable)	Current Balance	Required Monthly Payment
1. DIY Furniture	28.8%	$4,000	$1,500	$45
2. ABC Bank Credit Card	18.5%	$5,000	$2,000	$60 (3% of Bal.)
3. FAB Car Loan	7%	n/a	$23,000	$475
4. XYZ Bank Line of Credit	6% (Prime + 3%)	$25,000	$12,500	$250 (2% of Bal.)
		TOTAL	$39,000	$830

Next, plan your debt repayment strategy using three simple steps:

Step 1: Combine to Reduce Your Number of Debts

Where possible, transfer your higher interest debts over to your lower interest products. In the example, the higher interest DIY Furniture and ABC Bank Credit Card could be transferred to the XYZ Bank Line of Credit. This may seem obvious, but we often don't think of it. We get too busy just making our required payments. In the example, the transfer will cut the number of debts by 50% and will save hundreds of dollars in interest.

Step 2: Renegotiate to Minimize Your Interest Charges

Interest rates are negotiable. Try going back to your lender to negotiate lower rates on your remaining credit cards, loans, or lines of credit. You may not have received the best possible rate when you first received the financing and your credit may be stronger today. It can take just a phone call to reduce your rate significantly. You need to ask for a great rate to get one.

Step 3: Target to Maximize Your Results

Once you have reduced the number of debts you have to juggle and negotiated with lenders to minimize the interest on your remaining debt, your final task is to choose your target. Your debt target is the remaining debt with the highest interest rate. You will get a greater bang for your buck by throwing any extra dollars you can commit to the debt with the highest Annual Percentage Rate (APR). When that debt has been paid, redirect those dollars, in addition to the payment you are already making, to your debt with the next highest interest rate. Targeting your debts from highest to lowest interest rate saves the most money.

Notes

5th thing Investing IN Retirement Is Different from Investing FOR Retirement

by

Jim Yih

CSA, RDB, PRP

You can't talk about retirement without having some discussion about investing money. Investing is a well-covered topic of discussion with articles, books, advertisements and ideas widely available on how to invest money. Many of these ideas can fuel your passion to get rich fast because we live in a world of immediate returns and immediate rewards. Think about some of the common advertising slogans: *"Just add water," "Microwave ready in 2 minutes," "Lose weight in 7 days!," "30 minutes or it's free!"* and in the financial industry, *"Get rich quick!"* Wouldn't we all want to get rich quick?

When it comes to investment products, there is no shortage of choice or opportunities. And as a result, it is very easy for investors to become confused amid all this clutter.

INVESTMENT CHALLENGES FOR RETIREES

In the 1980's investment decisions for retirees were easier to make. Retirees could put their savings in safe, guaranteed investments with no risk and enjoy double-digit returns. In the 1990's, however, interest rates fell by 75% and all investors, including retirees, had to look to riskier investments to try and increase returns. Even with low inflation of 2% during the past decade, few retirees could afford to earn only 3 to 5% on their investments.

Looking to the future, retirees are likely to continue to face similar issues. Many retirees cannot afford not to take risks with capital if interest rates remain at low single-digit levels. As a result, they will continue to seek alternative investments to enhance returns with as little risk as possible. Unfortunately, higher returns bring more risk and we will continue to see more and more retirees, with investments exposed to a higher level of risk than they may want or need.

The goal of effective retirement planning is to create balance around the issues of money and life. A good retirement plan should include a process of evaluation of the assets you hold and the risk you are exposed to in your retirement portfolio.

WE NEED A NEW APPROACH TO INVESTING

Most people would agree that as you get older and closer to retirement, it makes sense to shift investments from being risky to more conservative. Chances are your personal circumstances after age 60 will be a lot different than when you were in your 30's. A retiree, for example, is more likely to want to supplement cash flow with income from investment whereas a young adult would be more interested in growing capital and having income compounded (added to the investment). The difference in lifestyle should prompt investors to make changes to their portfolios and strategies as they approach retirement. Although this seems to make sense, it does not seem to be practiced.

Investing for Retirement

The period of our lives when we are trying to build wealth through saving and investing is called **The Accumulation Phase.** From an investment perspective, it is not uncommon for people in the Accumulation Phase to invest for growth of capital. The financial industry has done a good job teaching people how to invest for retirement as you can hear in the principles and theories of investing such as:

Dollar Cost Averaging - a systematic approach of investing a fixed dollar amount at regular intervals (usually monthly) in a particular investment regardless of its share price. In this way, more shares are purchased when prices are low and fewer shares are bought when prices are high.

Diversification - the old theory of managing risk by not keeping all your eggs in one basket.

Long-Term Investing - a strategy that is preached by many advisors because long-term investing allows investors to ride out the unavoidable ups and downs of the market.

Relationship of Risk and Return - the concept that risk and return move together. As much as we would love investments that provide low risk with high returns, the reality is that higher returns bring more risk and lower risk investments generally have lower returns.

Buy and Hold - a long-term investment strategy based on the concept that in the long run financial markets give a good rate of return despite periods of volatility or decline.

Since these strategies and philosophies (and others) are well documented and well covered in popular literature, let's focus on how investing in retirement might be different than all these messages you hear.

In the Accumulation Phase, common sense would say that you invest money to make money. As a result, the investment industry has become a results-oriented industry. Investors are happy when they make money on their investments and the more, the better. On the other hand, they are not happy when they lose money.

Investing in Retirement

At retirement, we enter a new phase - **The Retirement Financial Phase.** The goal of this period should be very different from the goal of building wealth. It is a time when we begin to shift our thinking from saving to spending. If you don't, you may run the risk of dying with too much money and paying too much tax when you die. That means we would shift our investment mindset from growth to income. Instead of growing capital we would be looking to preserve or even spend capital. Portfolios would move from pre-authorized chequing plans (PACs) (where funds are transferred from personal accounts to investment accounts) to systematic withdrawal plans (SWPs) (where cash flow comes to your operating account from your investments on a planned basis). *"To achieve this, there should also be a shift in thinking away from the need for higher returns in order to manage risk."*

Higher return on investment is the goal of every investor regardless of what stage of life he or she is in. It is my observation that through the course of retirement, returns grow less important and other issues like the simplicity of managing money, control over income, personal health and quality of life become more important.

The rule is simple: risk and return go hand in hand. The higher the returns, the greater the risk, and conversely the lower the risk, the lower the returns.

Many retirees don't realize that higher returns can sometimes mean more tax in the future. Higher returns can also lead to unintentional outcomes such as dying with too much money. A good beginning step to planning investment for retirement is to write out the changes you expect in your financial and lifestyle objectives once you are retired.

Old habits are hard to break. The following are some typical situations why portfolios don't change as people get closer to retirement:

- ~ Retirees who think and invest as if they are still in the Accumulation Phase and who are primarily saving and investing for growth.

- ~ Retirees who have been reluctant to spend their portfolios only to find they reach an age where they can't (or won't) spend their money.

- ~ Retirees who continue with similar portfolios to what they had before they retired.

All these types of people may be continuing to save for that rainy day that never comes.

In my experience as a financial advisor, I have found it very difficult to shift people from being savers to spenders. Perhaps it is because everyone is fearful of running out of money. It is not different from trying to turn a spender into a saver. In either case, change does not happen overnight.

From a portfolio or investment perspective, many retirees are focused on trying to get higher returns but for the wrong reasons. If retirement is about lifestyle, and trying to live the best years of your life, the goal should be about spending not saving. It should be about spending capital not growing capital. It should be about protecting your money and not risking it.

Retirement should be a time when you feel financially independent and in control of your financial decisions. Unfortunately for many retirees, they are too exposed to things they can't control like the stock market. As a result, when the market goes through a correction or crashes, retirees may have to delay retirement or even go back to work.

In my mind, this is not a sound retirement plan because it means you never have control over when you are going to retire. In order to establish a sense of freedom, independence, control and predictability, you need to change the way you think about investing and your portfolio may need to change accordingly.

Here are three guidelines that can help you protect your retirement assets from market corrections and investment mistakes in retirement.

IN RETIREMENT, TAKE THE TIME TO UNDERSTAND RISK

Once upon a time, close to your first birthday, you let go of your mother's hand and launched yourself across the room. You might have fallen flat on your face, but the thrill of discovering a whole new world was worth the risk.

You've acquired a lot of experience about risk since then: riding a bicycle; driving a car; asking for that first date; getting that first loan; or starting a brand new career. Investing is another beginning and another risk for many people. Some consider themselves risk-takers. Others tend to be more conservative or *"risk-averse."*

I believe risk is the foundation of all investment decisions, and it is especially important for the conservative investor to understand and appreciate it. This leads us to a key principle for successful investing: Understand, manage and accept risk in order to minimize and avoid surprises.

What Is Risk?

From an investment perspective, there are two definitions of risk. One definition is held by the investment industry, the other by the investor. In order to fully appreciate risk, you need to understand both.

Investment Industry's Definition of Risk

The industry defines risk in terms of standard deviation or volatility. In other words, how much will an investment fluctuate between its highs and lows? If it fluctuates a lot, it's highly volatile and therefore riskier. If it fluctuates only a little, it's less volatile and probably safer.

When advisors talk about risk with their clients, they also speak in terms of volatility - how much a fund fluctuates from the average - the swings from high to low. But that's not what concerns the investor. What concerns the investor is:

"Could I lose my capital, and if so, how much?"

Investor's Definition of Risk

The investor defines risk as the dictionary does, i.e. *"to expose oneself to the chance of loss."* For example, if you provide venture capital or risk capital to a project, you expect (and hope) to realize a profitable return. Backers of Broadway shows face enormous risk of loss. For every successful **Phantom of the Opera**, another show closes after only a few performances. There are no guarantees of success.

It's true that volatility and chance of loss often go hand in hand. For example, a fund that fluctuates a great deal is also likely to experience a higher probability of loss but this may not always be the case.

BE MINDFUL OF YOUR RISK CAPACITY

When it comes to investing, risk cannot be ignored. The problem is we place much more emphasis on analyzing past performance than risk, and quite often risk is ignored altogether.

How much risk are you willing to take? That's the question every financial advisor and institution will ask you because they are regulated to do so. It is likely that the answer to that question can be expressed by a few words like conservative, moderate, aggressive or some variation of these generic terms. Nowadays, financial advisors and institutions have you complete questionnaires to measure your tolerance for risk. At the end of the questionnaire, you are then lumped into one of five or six categories of investors and your investments are selected based on the results. I think these questionnaires are fine for investing for retirement but there should be separate questionnaires geared for investing in retirement. Investing in retirement should be based more on risk capacity as opposed to risk tolerance.

Risk tolerance is the amount of risk you WANT to take. Risk capacity, on the other hand, is the amount of risk you NEED to take. Most of the industry focus is on risk tolerance but it is so important to be mindful of risk capacity.

Although we may perceive risk tolerance and risk capacity to be very similar, they can be very different. While the industry does a good job of asking about your risk tolerance, there are three issues:

~ Risk tolerance is completely subjective. It often comes from feelings and emotions as opposed to logic.

~ There are no universal definitions of risk tolerance. Risk means different things to different people. Ask two different people about how risky they are and they might use the same word to define their risk tolerance. For example, you might get a 35-year-old and a 70-year-old both saying that they have conservative risk tolerances, but the 70-year-old has a very different definition from the 35-year-old of what conservative means. Conservative investing is an abused term because, like the term *"risk"*, there are no universal definitions.

~ A person's risk tolerance is always changing. How much risk you want to take can change depending on how you are feeling that day. For example, on a bad day, you might feel more risk-averse. It is also very common to see investors with higher risk tolerances when markets are strong because they see the benefits of risk. On the other hand, when markets are struggling, those same investors tend to have a lower tolerance for risk because no one likes to lose money.

Risk capacity is a better measure when evaluating personal risk because it requires some work, analysis and thought before you can come up with an answer. To determine your risk capacity, you really have to look at your financial situation and do some planning for the future.

Using an example of two very different brothers, Henry and Sam, let me illustrate the issue.

Henry is 58 and what some would call a natural saver. He is married to Becca (another saver) and they have two kids. Henry and Becca are both successful professionals with higher than average incomes and, as a result of their prudent financial strategies, they have over a million dollars in investible assets. In addition, their home is paid off and they own recreational property and investment property.

Sam on the other hand is 54 and prefers to live by the motto *"live for today."* Although Sam makes an above-average income, he saves very little because he spends most of what he makes. He eats out every day, takes two or three vacations a year, and has a passion for nice cars and designer clothes. Sam is in his second marriage and in his words, *"he is still paying for his first marriage."* Sam has about $25,000 saved in RRSPs.

As you can see, Sam and Henry are in very different financial situations. While the example may seem extreme, it illustrates the point that they can easily have the same risk tolerance but given their financial picture, they have very different capacities for risk.

Henry does not need to take any risks at all. He could invest all his money into boring but safe guaranteed investments at 2% to 4% and still live very comfortably in retirement. In fact, he could stick it in a mattress or a sock drawer and still be set for the future.

Sam on the other hand probably needs to take some risks in his portfolio because he has not saved enough for his retirement. You see, risk tolerance, although important, is really secondary to risk capacity.

To understand your personal risk tolerance and risk capacity will require some self-discovery and general financial planning. I like to think of investing as one piece of the puzzle. On its own this piece does not have a lot of meaning, but once you find the pieces around it, it starts to make some sense. When the whole puzzle fits together, then decisions become a lot easier to make. Make sure you are investing your money by taking into consideration your total financial picture. Using large picture thinking will help you get a better sense of how much risk you need to take.

If you are not sure how to do this, any financial advisor should be able to sit down with you and figure out your risk tolerance and risk capacity.

RETIREES MUST BE AWARE OF THE RETIREMENT RISK ZONE

My bias is that people NEED to be more conservative with their portfolios as they approach retirement and especially when they are drawing income from their portfolios in retirement. This belief flows out of the **Retirement Risk Zone**.

The Retirement Risk Zone is the critical period leading into and just after retirement. Some have said it is the three to five years before retirement and the three to five years after retirement. Potential short-term portfolio losses due to markets during this time can have significant long-term effects on how long capital in the portfolio will last.

Average Returns Can Be Misleading

Most financial and retirement planning is done using average return assumptions. For example, Peter is 65 years old and his retirement plan assumes that his portfolio over a long period of time will generate a 7% return. The problem is Peter can't get a 7% Guaranteed Investment Certificate (GIC) these days. Instead, Peter invests in a balanced portfolio of stocks, bonds and cash to try to achieve his goal of 7%. Peter is not unlike most people these days reverting to mutual funds, stocks and other managed portfolios to try to enhance returns.

Although I have seen some balanced portfolios and mutual funds achieve long-term average returns of 7%, I have not seen any consistent returns of 7%. In other words, a portfolio that is exposed to the market does not make 7% each and every year. Instead, it might make 27% one year and then lose 13% the next year to average 7%. It is these ups and downs that are real to investors.

Sequence Is Important

Most investors, including those in the Retirement Risk Zone, are exposed to market changes. It is crucial that investors are aware that the sequence of returns can have a dramatic effect on the longevity of their portfolios.

Let's say Peter earns a 7% return on his portfolio but withdraws 9% each and every year. If we assume that a 7% return is consistent every year, he will run out of money by age 86. His money lasts 21 years. This straight-line thinking is exactly how most projections work in the financial industry. The problem is that this type of calculation, based on this straight-line thinking, is creating misleading projections for clients.

Year	1	2	3	4	5	6	7	8	9	10	11	12
Scenario 1	7%	7%	7%	7%	7%	7%	7%	7%	7%	7%	7%	7%
Scenario 2	27%	7%	-13%	27%	7%	-13%	27%	7%	-13%	27%	7%	-13%
Scenario 3	-13%	27%	7%	-13%	27%	7%	-13%	27%	7%	-13%	27%	7%

Let's compare that to a different scenario where Peter invests some of his money in the markets. In the first year, he makes 27%; the second year he makes 7%; the third year he loses 13%; and then the cycle repeats itself (year 4 he makes 27%, year 5 he makes 7% and year 6 he loses 13% . . .). The average return is still 7% but this sequence of returns allows the money to last an additional nine years to age 95. Basically a couple of good years off the start can make a huge difference to the longevity of the portfolio.

Now if a couple of good years adds to the longevity of a portfolio, what would happen if you experienced some negative returns early on? Let's look at a third scenario where Peter starts the first year with a

13% loss. Then in the second year he makes 27%, the third year he makes 7% and the cycle repeats itself. You probably recognize these are the same returns as the second scenario but just in a different order. This sequence of returns produces the same average return of 7% but now the portfolio only lasts 16 years. The portfolio runs out 14 years earlier than if Peter had the good returns in the first couple of years.

So what does this all mean for Peter? How long his $100,000 lasts, really depends on good timing or bad timing. I believe good planning should be a little more predictable and that is why I recommend to Canadians that they need to spend a lot more time on risk than just completing a questionnaire. In my experience retirees need to take less risk than they think - especially if they want more predictability and control in retirement.

As soon as you plan to take income from your investments, risk should decrease. One might argue that you still have time for recovery if the markets change but taking income will accelerate portfolio losses and can reduce the amount of time you have to take income from capital.

A FINAL THOUGHT

For some investors, the need for higher returns seems to be a priority but how would you know unless you took the time to run some projections using variable returns instead of straight-line returns? The risk-return problem is compounded by low interest rates but sometimes slow and steady investing actually wins the race.

In my opinion, the risk continuum has swung too far in the direction of investing in risky investments. While I understand the merits of investing in stocks and mutual funds at younger ages, I think too many people, especially retirees, are taking more risk than they need to.

Evaluate your portfolio and find out how much you have invested in non-guaranteed investments like mutual funds and stocks. If you have a greater proportion of non-guaranteed investments, recognize three important issues:

1. More stocks mean less control. Your timing may be a case of good timing or bad timing so retirement planning might be more like a game of rolling the dice. Roll a 1, 3, 4 or 6 and you will be just fine. Roll a 2 or a 5 and you might have to delay retirement, cut your expenses or go back to work. Can you imagine relying on dice to plan for your retirement?

2. More stocks mean less predictability. The whole idea of retirement planning is to look into the future and create as predictable a scenario as possible. It's never perfect but planning means you are creating a future by design and not by accident. The key to planning with mutual funds and stocks is to recognize that the math used to calculate returns always happens in straight lines which will never happen in reality. Run multiple projections including projections showing worst-case scenarios. For those using financial advisors, ask for returns using Monte Carlo Analysis (which is a software program that applies variable returns instead of straight-line returns).

3. Ask your advisor or financial institution how much you are paying in fees. It's been well documented that fees are a big determinant of investment performance. Also ask how much your advisor is getting paid. A significant portion of the total fees goes to pay your financial advisor. That's not a bad thing if you have a good and attentive advisor but how would you know if you never asked the question? High fees mean less money in your pocket. Be aware that, in most cases, advisors get paid more to sell you mutual funds and stocks as opposed to GICs and other guaranteed investments. It is a potential conflict of interest that may or may not exist.

In summary, we all know that investing has its fair share of ups and downs. In retirement, the downs can be really tough when drawing income from the portfolio. Your objective is to recognize when you need to change from investing for retirement to investing in retirement.

Before you retire, take the time to re-evaluate your portfolio and your specific needs in retirement. Will you be investing to spend your money? Do you really want to preserve your capital and, if so, what for? How much risk do you need to take and how much risk do you want to take?

Hindsight Is Perfect Planning!
Rein Selles

I f you were to look back on the decisions of your life, would you have acted differently? It is said that hindsight is 20/20 vision - everything we should have known or could have done is laid out perfectly.

Learning occurs more frequently with error than it does with success. That means, most of us should be learning a lot about our own risk tolerance and our investment choices as we make one mistake after another. One difference you may have noticed in learning from financial errors is that the playing field is not the same when a new choice is made. So, even though I may be wiser on my next investment, the context for my decision changes and now I find myself in the same position of loss as I was before.

Chapter 5 reminds me of the results of a study reported by an American chaplain on a visit to Canada about 10 years ago. The chaplain told the audience that a group of 45 senior adults who had lived long lives were asked,

> *"If you could live your life over again, what would you do differently?"*

There were three common responses in the group:

> ~ *"If I had known I would live this long, I would have had more fun!"*

For me, this is the best interpretation of the meaning of *"risk."* Our ability to grow and experience life is directly related to the willingness to step out on a limb - whether that is in our financial affairs, interpersonal relationships or personal growth.

~ *"If I had known I would live this long, I would have thought about it!"*

If every decision has a consequence at some later point in our lives, the models for making effective decisions should incorporate a great deal more thought about how a choice made today could have implications well into retirement.

~ *"If I had known I would live this long, I would have invested in something that would last beyond my lifetime!"*

In our pursuit of money we forget that money is only a means by which we create memories - good ones and bad ones. The real risk is that we can live life so focused on immediate gain that we lose the real value in the relationships that will mean the most to us as life ends.

Early in my career I had the opportunity to meet a famous and very wealthy Canadian in Ontario. If you looked at his home, the furniture and vehicles, you could easily assume that he had it all! In fact, he was confined to his bed and the only human contact he had was with the nurses who cared for him. Where were his family and friends? Lost. And, if you visit nursing homes across this country, you will find many elderly in the same position.

I am of the school of balanced choices. Enough money to make the memories possible. That means the risk has to be appropriate to the goal.

Goal Setting Your Retirement Savings

Patricia French

G oal setting is a particularly effective tool for targeting savings. We do this task reasonably well before retirement. We save for specific goals in keeping with our stage in the lifecycle: a wedding, a down payment on our first home, new vehicles, vacations, and children's education. These are specific, measurable, attainable, realistic goals that evoke a clear blueprint to achievement. We also save for RETIREMENT! This goal is rather nebulous and elusive when we begin saving. We attempt to make the goal more clear-cut by using various *"rules of thumb"* to ensure we build *"enough"* wealth. Save 10% of your gross income. Save 20% if you want to be wealthy. Subtract your age from 100 to determine the percentage of your investment dollars you should have invested in equities. And the list goes on...

Retirement is unlike your earlier goals. Retirement is its own epoch with an indeterminate timeframe punctuated with undiscovered interests, newfound opportunities, and unforeseen issues. The unknown drives us to save and to think that if this much savings is good, more must be better. It also promotes the mindset to minimize spending today, just in case we need it more down the road.

In retirement you may struggle to spend the money saved. Is that because it wasn't clear what you planned to use it for? I understand it was intended for retirement, but what does that really mean? It is akin to saying we're saving to buy a *"lifestyle,"* which could feel like a somewhat ambiguous goal. We weren't specific about how we would use the savings once retired. We simply tried to build the biggest pile we could. Will you use your savings to regularly supplement your other retirement income? Or do you see your savings as your *"fun money"* to use for travel, renovation, or gifts? Or will it be a little of both?

Knowing how you plan to use your retirement investment income helps with formulating your retirement investment plan. Investing seems to cause feelings of stress and anxiety for many people, especially when the market is on the decline. On the other hand, euphoria, confidence, and greed can plague investors when the market is climbing with no end in sight.

Ideally, your retirement investment plan is constructed to shelter you from risk you cannot absorb. So the money you can't live without is safe. Safety, just like risk, is a relative term. When discussing investing, an advisor friend of mine will ask clients whether they think jumping out of a plane is risky. When most admit they think so, he trumps them by saying that he neglected to tell them the plane was still on the ground. Do they now see the risk differently? Of course they do. With more information we can better gauge the risk our investments present. You are wise to get the facts by doing your own research or speaking with a professional advisor you trust, because your investment plan in retirement may involve complex decisions with relative uncertainty. We cannot know what will happen going forward, so we are left with having to make some assumptions. In the 50 years leading to 2008 there have been 12 bear markets (declining) and 11 bull markets (rising). It is reasonable to expect you will ride through a few of these market cycles over a 30-year retirement. How much these cycles will affect you depends on your investment portfolio.

"The four most expensive words in the English language are, 'This time it's different'."
~ SIR JOHN TEMPLETON

More flexibility in your retirement plan could mean more willingness or ability to accept investment risk. Conventional investment wisdom deems a long-term time horizon to be appropriate for mitigating volatility in the market. Retirement could be considered long-term since it could last 30 years or more for many. The problem is that losses in the market occur and if they coincide with retirement they can radically diminish investment income. If that would only impact the number of vacations you can take a year, it may be a risk you can live with. If decreased investment income could affect groceries, then it's not worth the chance of loss.

People who start saving later for retirement feel pressured to make big gains to catch up. Panic mode can set in for people who lost money when invested aggressively and are trying to recover.

Some people realize too late that they have not saved enough. In my work, I have seen the effect of financial strain on individuals and couples. Doing some homework on retirement needs can temper doubts of not having enough and ease the pressure to tolerate higher investment risk while retired.

Do you know what your pension income (employment pension, CPP, and OAS) will be in retirement? Have you written a budget and do you know what your lifestyle will cost? Does your pension income cover your lifestyle? You'll feel compelled to maximize investment returns even in retirement if you do not have a firm grasp of your income and expense needs in retirement.

People often adjust their retirement plans when the market goes off course or their circumstances change. How easy this would be for you is partially dependent on how flexible you are willing to be with your plan. You could call it contingency financial planning. What would you be willing to do if the investment portion of your retirement income were to decline? What lifestyle expenditures in your budget would you be prepared to sacrifice to some degree? Would you be open to returning to the paid workforce, even part-time or on contract?

If your plans are not open to negotiation, then safety, not return, wins. While that may mean less money than a more aggressive investment strategy, at least with reasonable certainty, you'll finish the race.

Exercise Seven

Making It Personal
Risk Capacity

The idea behind determining risk capacity is to help make investment decisions based more on financial ability and needs rather than risk tolerance which focuses more on emotions and wants.

Investment decisions are more of an art than a science because there is no such thing as perfection. As a result, this exercise serves as a guideline. In each step there is room to enhance or depress your scores as required.

Step 1: Start with your age. The old rule of thumb is to take your age and that number should represent the percentage of investments that should be in safer, more conservative investments. Given this rule of thumb, the older you are, the more conservative you should be.

WHAT IS YOUR AGE?
Your age serves as the starting number of points and reflects the percentage of your total investments that should be invested safely. If your age is 55, then 55% of your portfolio should be invested in fixed income sources like bonds, GICs or cash.

_____ 66 %

Step 2: How much time do you have? The more time you have until you retire, the further you are from drawing income from your investments. If you are 10 years or more from retirement, then you can handle more risk by reducing the amount of fixed income investments in the portfolio. Conversely, the closer you are to retirement, the more conservative you need to be.

Guidelines:

~ More than 10 years to retirement   subtract 5 points

~ 5 to 10 years to retirement   add 5 points

~ Less than 5 years to retirement   add 5 to 10 points

~ Already retired   add 10 points or more

HOW MANY POINTS DO YOU GET FOR TIME   _10_

Step 3: Are you drawing income from your investments? As soon as you are drawing income from your portfolio, risk or volatility can do a lot of damage to the portfolio. When retirees start drawing income, they should be more conservative with their portfolios.

Guidelines:

~ If you are not drawing income from your investments   make no adjustment

~ If you are just spending the income or growth and preserving capital   add 5 to 10 points

~ If you are spending growth & capital   add 10 to 25 points

~ If you cannot live without this income (from the investments),   add another 5 to 10 points

HOW MANY POINTS DO YOU GET FOR INCOME   _0_

Step 4: How is your financial stability? When it comes to risk tolerance, the more stable you are, the more risk you can afford to take. But when it comes to risk capacity, the more financially stable you are, the less risk you need to take. In other words, start with risk capacity and then make adjustments if you want to take risks. The tricky part of this step is if you are not financially stable. In that case you could argue that you should not take as much risk because you may need access to the capital. On the other hand you could also argue you need to take more risks in order to achieve retirement goals.

Guidelines:

~ If you are financially stable (income greater than expenses, saving regularly, debt under control, managing investments)   add 5 to 15 points

~ If you are not sure   make no adjustments

HOW MANY POINTS DO YOU GET FOR FINANCIAL STABILITY   _5_

Step 5: What returns do you need to achieve? The only way you can answer this question properly is if you have taken the time to develop a financial plan or a retirement plan. All plans require a certain set of assumptions for rate of return and that number will influence how much risk you need to take in the portfolio.

Guidelines:

~	If you need to earn 3% or less	add 15 to 25 points
~	If you need to earn 3% to 5%	add 10 to 20 points
~	If you need to earn 5% to 7%	add 0 to 10 points
~	If you need to earn 7% to 10%	subtract 0 to 10 points
~	If you need to earn more than 10%	subtract 5 to 15 points

HOW MANY POINTS DO YOU GET FOR RETURN   *10*

Final Score   *9 1*

Add up the numbers from the five steps and this number should reflect the percentage of your portfolio that should be invested in fixed-income investments. For example, a retired, financially stable 62-year-old female drawing income from her portfolio would have a risk capacity of 70 to 90. That means she should not take a lot of risks and 70 to 90% of her portfolio should be invested in more conservative investments like bonds, GICs or cash. She could have a much higher risk tolerance but that would be her choice to take more risks.

Notes

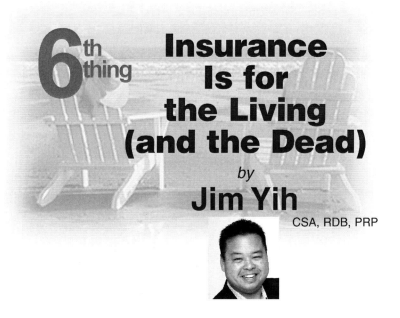

6th thing
Insurance Is for the Living (and the Dead)
by
Jim Yih
CSA, RDB, PRP

L ife insurance has always been a controversial and often negative topic of discussion. The roots of this negativity stem from the stereotype of the plaid suit salesman, who goes from door to door pitching the merits of life insurance. Traditionally, it was more about making the sale than incorporating life insurance into a comprehensive financial plan.

Critics of life insurance have also questioned the commissions that agents make. In some cases, life insurance sales can result in payment of substantial commissions and bonuses. To be fair, there are some life insurance products that pay more commissions than others. Today, the role of life insurance agents has changed from slick salesmen to professional advisors who incorporate insurance into a personal financial or retirement plan.

I have not met many people who enjoy paying for life insurance. It seems to be one of those optional necessities in the world of personal finance. In many cases, we know we need it but we may also hate setting aside funds for it.

Life insurance is what I term the *"unselfish benefit"* in that those who purchase life insurance may not be the ones who reap the true rewards of the product. One of the best ways to determine if you need insurance is to put yourself in the shoes of the beneficiary of the policy when you die - think of yourself as the survivor.

DO YOU NEED LIFE INSURANCE IN RETIREMENT?

In our workshops, a frequent question is, *"Do you still need life insurance in retirement?"* This question may sound easy to tackle but it may be more complicated than you think. Some common issues include:

~ People who have bought older whole life or universal life policies and who are wondering if retirement means cashing out these policies for their cash values.

~ People who are retiring and who face the dilemma of converting group life insurance policies into personal plans.

~ People who have term insurance policies renewing in retirement and are wondering if it makes sense to continue paying higher premiums to keep the coverage.

~ People who are wondering about other kinds of insurance like critical illness and long-term care insurance policies and whether these policies for the living are more appropriate in retirement.

The biggest problem with life insurance is that it involves emotion which is not always the best way to make important decisions. It's not easy to look into the future and envision a life that will be lived without you.

The purpose of life insurance may have seemed clear when you were younger and wanted to ensure resources would be available to support your spouse, raise and educate your children, and pay off debts. Life insurance was a means to create an instant estate to allow your loved-ones to carry on financially should you pass away.

Many experts have argued that the greatest need for insurance is when you are young and that the best form of insurance that fits the need during that period is term insurance. While there is some truth to this general rule of thumb there may also be value to insurance in later life.

Insurance in Retirement

Just like cereal and milk or strawberries and whipped cream, life insurance and estate planning go really well together. While protection of dependents is the most obvious reason for insurance, there are other situations where life insurance in retirement may also make sense.

To Pay off Debts – In the past, retirement decisions were generally deferred until all debts were paid. Today, however, we live in times where debt is abundant, and increasingly Canadians are retiring with more debt than in the past. This debt comes in many different forms such as lines of credit, credit cards and even mortgages. If you are carrying debt in retirement, then life insurance can be used to pay off those debts at death rather than forcing your survivors to liquidate assets. Alternatively if you have enough liquid savings or assets to pay off debts to the estate, then life insurance may not be necessary.

To Cover Taxes at Death – At the moment you die, you are deemed to have sold all your assets. As a result, there may be a substantial tax bill to the estate as a result of income from registered plans (RRSPs or RRIFs), capital gains from investment portfolios, real estate dispositions and other sources of income. Life insurance can be used to ensure there is money in the estate to pay for this tax liability. Keep in mind that the government will still get paid its share of tax. Keeping your Life Insurance means your beneficiaries will get more of the value of the estate because the insurance creates cash to pay for the tax bill.

To Cover Final Expenses like Funeral Expenses and Legal Fees – Every estate has expenses, but where will the money come from to pay for these expenses? It is crucial to ensure there is enough liquid cash to pay for fees and expenses. For some, life insurance can be a great way to inject liquid cash into the estate.

To Provide Income for Your Dependents – Generally, the plan in retirement would assume that dependents have moved out of your home but, as the last Canadian Census showed, children are staying home longer or leaving and then returning with a spouse and your grandchildren. The dependent in retirement, however, may be your spouse and not the kids. Will your spouse need your income when you pass away? If he or she needs some or all of your income to make ends meet, then you are a likely candidate for life insurance in retirement unless you have significant savings or assets to leave behind. Before you proceed on this issue remember the best way to work through this is to simply think of yourself as the survivor.

To Leave a Larger Estate for Your Beneficiaries – Canadians and their advisors have joked that the ideal strategy is to spend your money so you can die broke! The flaw with this strategy, of course, is that you never know when you are going to die. Most people could never die broke because running out of money is the biggest fear they face in life. In fact, leaving money to your spouse, kids, grandkids or others is not a bad goal. The goal of leaving money can reflect relationships and create legacies. Life insurance is a great way to pass money on to the people you love on a tax-free basis.

To Equalize Your Estate – Life insurance can create a pool of cash to allow your executor to make things equal for your beneficiaries when some things can't be divided. One common example is where real estate is involved. For example, you might have a family cottage that is really only being used by one of three children. If the cottage is willed to the three kids, there is a good chance that the one child who uses the cottage will have to buy out the other two siblings, but where will the cash come from? Life insurance is a method to equalize the estate by giving the cottage to the child who wants it and giving cash equal to the value of the cottage through a life insurance policy to the other two children.

To Help Corporations and Business Arrangements Remain Viable – There are many uses for life insurance and estate planning when a business is involved. Every situation is unique and should involve a team of professionals.

To Provide for Charities – Most often when we donate money to charities, we do it in the form of a direct contribution. Typically, someone knocks on your door or solicits you through the phone. Sometimes, we give a little by leaving our change at the cash register or even by attending a fundraiser of some sort. Charitable gifting with life insurance is much different. The most attractive advantage of using life insurance is that it allows you to make a much larger gift to a charity. In addition to the goodwill, giving to a charity through your estate can save a lot of money in taxes.

Obviously, this list is not exhaustive but it does represent some of the key uses of life insurance in the retirement planning process. The greatest benefit of having life insurance in your plan is that the proceeds are paid to your beneficiaries on a tax-free basis.

WHEN SHOULD YOU GET RID OF EXISTING LIFE INSURANCE?

There is a golden rule, *"Only buy insurance if you need it."* If you don't need it in retirement, then get rid of it.

Before You Cancel . . .

Before you cancel life insurance make sure you've considered all the options because you only have one chance to make the right decision. Once you cancel, it's really tough or even impossible to get it back. Here are some important things to think about before you cancel your life insurance policy:

Talk to Your Beneficiaries – Before cancelling insurance, it may make sense to have a discussion with your beneficiaries about whether they want to keep the policy in place and pay for the premiums. Paying the premiums of the insurance to keep the policy may be one of the best investments your beneficiaries ever make. Open up the lines of communication about two tough topics – death and money.

Talk to Your Spouse – If you have a spouse, he or she is likely to be the key beneficiary of your life insurance policy. Have a good, realistic discussion about whether your spouse will need capital when you pass away.

Get a Medical Examination – The feasibility and cost of life insurance all depends on life expectancy. If you go and get a complete medical check-up and discover your life expectancy might be shorter than you thought, you may want to think twice about cancelling your insurance. Life insurance is one of those things that is easy to get when you are healthy and really tough to get when you are not.

Consider Converting Group Insurance – If you participated in a group plan, when you leave work, you are likely to have an option to convert your group life insurance benefit into a personal policy. A complete check-up will also help you make the right decision. If you are not healthy, then you may want to consider converting the group insurance into a personal policy because it provides coverage without underwriting. If you are healthy and need insurance, you may be better off by seeking a personal policy for a more cost-effective price.

Consider Keeping Whole Life and Universal Life Policies – It is tough to replace permanent policies because they become more valuable the longer you own them. Much of the costs occur in the early years. Later in life, it is difficult to replace these policies because you can never buy the insurance at a cheaper cost. Instead of cancelling older whole life or universal life policies, it may be prudent for your beneficiaries to evaluate the option to take over the payments on the policy. From a purely mathematical perspective, it could be a great investment for your beneficiaries since it is in their financial interest to keep the policy going for the death benefit.

Don't Wait until Costs Are too High – Remember, replacement insurance costs more the older you get. Waiting to make decisions till you retire might mean choices will be more limited due to costs.

INSURANCE FOR THE LIVING

The irony of life insurance is that the benefit is realized at the death of the policy holder. It is really *"death insurance"* but that would be a hard idea to sell. Today, the world of insurance has expanded to also provide benefits while the policy holders are alive – a living benefit.

Living benefit plans are insurance policies that provide financial benefits to survivors who face issues due to aging, illness and dependency. Two of the most common forms of living benefits are critical illness insurance and long-term care insurance. These two forms of insurance become more relevant once you are retired.

Critical Illness Insurance

The goal of insurance is to help you in times of need and to protect against risk of loss. Life insurance protects the survivor from the risk of financial hardship in the event of a loss of earnings. Disability insurance helps if you are unable to work due to a disability. Car insurance helps you if you get into an accident. Critical illness insurance is simply another type of insurance that helps you if you become critically ill. There are many different conditions that might be covered under a critical illness policy but the most common are heart attacks, strokes, and cancer.

When people get sick, their focus needs to be on getting better. Unfortunately, financial hardship can cause people to lose that focus. That's exactly where critical illness insurance comes into play.

Typically, critical illness insurance provides a lump sum payment when a specific condition is diagnosed. The money can then be used for whatever purposes make life easier. Some examples include finding alternative medical treatments anywhere in the world, hiring a caregiver, paying debts, covering expenses that are not covered under government health care, paying for private nursing homes, or providing income support.

Have you known of a friend, family member or colleague who had a stroke or heart attack, was diagnosed with cancer, Parkinson's, or Alzheimer's disease, or experienced kidney failure? Chances are you will have known somebody in your life who has become critically ill. The risks are real and the road to recovery can be a costly one.

What Should I Look for in Critical Illness Insurance?

Like any type of insurance, the benefit from the policy will only be realized if something goes wrong. Insurance is meant to protect against risk. Like any other type of insurance, I would encourage you to shop around for the best product for you.

Most life insurance companies will offer some variation of critical illness insurance. Remember, not all products are the same. There are differences in price, coverage, and the options you can select. Whenever you sign a contract, there is a need to check the fine print.

Because heart attacks, cancer, strokes and other illnesses are becoming more common, the likelihood of facing these illnesses is increasing. As a result, critical illness insurance is not inexpensive. Make sure you compare the details of the policies available from different companies and recognize that cheaper is not always better. See a qualified financial professional if you need help . . . preferably one that specializes in living benefit policies.

Long Term Care Insurance

The good news is we are living longer. The not-so-good news is we are living longer and as we age, the risk of illnesses such as Alzheimer's and dementia, diabetes, stroke, heart disease and cancer can increase. There is growing concern that Canadians will pay more long-term care costs out of their pockets in the future as support from government sources is eroded. Will future retirees have enough income and savings to pay for this care?

'What happens when I can no longer take care of myself?'

This is a concern many of us may face; and, this is where long-term care insurance comes in.

Long-term care insurance is another coverage that is rapidly growing in popularity. It pays a daily or monthly benefit for medical or custodial care received in a nursing facility, in a hospital, or at home if you are unable to carry out some of the common activities of daily living (ADLs). Some examples of ADLs include:

~ Bathing

~ Dressing and undressing

~ Eating

~ Transferring from bed to chair, and back

~ Voluntarily controlling urinary and fecal discharge

~ Using the toilet

~ Walking (not bedridden)

It is very important to apply for long-term care insurance while you are still healthy. This is especially important if there is a history of serious illness and longevity in your family. These policies are usually guaranteed renewable, meaning once you qualify, you remain eligible as long as the premiums are paid.

The premiums are based on your age at the time you purchase the insurance, and rates are usually locked-in for the life of the policy. Since most premiums for this type of insurance are paid with after-tax dollars, the long-term care insurance benefits are tax-free.

MY TWO CENTS

For some, the issue of having insurance in retirement can be really simple and for others, it is incredibly complex. Generally, retirement diminishes the need for life insurance. By evaluation, some may find that they do not need insurance but will decide to keep it anyway. For others, the need for insurance might change from life insurance to insurance for the living. The bottom line is that all the issues surrounding insurance are very personal. Health, life expectancy, money, family and lifestyle will all affect your desire or need to have insurance coverage in place.

Should you determine additional or a different type of insurance is needed, apply as young as you can to keep premiums lower and improve your chances of qualifying medically. At the end of the day, the fact that resources are limited may mean that life insurance or insurance for critical illness or long-term care are not options in retirement. Alternatively, the more savings and assets you have, the less you may need insurance.

Should insurance be needed, make sure you get it while you are younger because as you get older, you may not qualify for it or be able to afford it.

Just like anything else in life, not all life insurance products are created equal. That is especially true when it comes to price. Once you have an idea of what type of life insurance you need and how much you need, it is critically important to shop around for the best deal. If you are not sure how to accomplish that process, then seek advice from an independent insurance broker who can shop around for you.

Insurance Planning Is
a Good Rehearsal

Rein Selles

I remember the exact day that I recognized the true nature of life insurance. At the time I was in my late 30's and my wife and I had two children. Raised in a household where the male role was to *"take care of business"*, I made sure, at the time of our marriage, that I had life insurance. The capital, paid at death, would ensure that my spouse would always have the means to create income for a period of time.

I was watching her manage the needs of the children and suddenly realized that, if she died, I would be the one who was vulnerable since there was no policy on her life. As the survivor, I would face two choices:

~ Stay at home and care for the children but forfeit the means of support for the family; or

~ Continue to work out of the home and use limited resources to hire that support during working hours.

The sense that *"insurance is for the living"* suddenly meant something. While it was my responsibility to ensure that life insurance would be paid to my wife, it was my comfort to know, in the event of my wife's death, I had the means to maintain my lifestyle as the survivor.

From a professional perspective, I have worked with a number of clients (male and female) who are the survivors of relationships. Their need for professional advice came in the recognition that, while their partner had provided for the needs, they had not prepared them to manage on their own. In some cases, survivors had never developed a financial identity, learned basic financial skills or worked with advisors and institutions.

The sense of loss of the relationship experienced by the survivor is compounded by the realization that the tools needed for maintaining financial security may have been lost as well. I issue a warning to all couples at workshops:

> *"If you leave the details of your plan to another, what happens to your plan when that person walks away or is no longer available to provide the details?"*

Here are the stage directions for your rehearsal as a survivor of a relationship:

~ You know what income will continue at death and where it will come from.

~ You know what capital will be paid from corporate or personal policies and have the knowledge as to its initial placement and investment until advice is forthcoming.

~ You know you have to apply for Canada Pension survivor benefits.

~ You know all the expenses (not just those you pay for).

~ You are confident that the combination of capital and income paid or created will be sufficient to maintain your lifestyle.

If you can't respond positively to these questions, share them with your partner and take the time together to teach and learn. No amount of money from insurance can take the place of what you will learn.

Insurance Should Be
Bought - Not Sold
Patricia French

Insurance needs should be reassessed within the context of your overall financial plan for retirement. As consumers of insurance products, we often surrender to a get-it-and-forget-it mindset. We purchase the insurance policy and then cross *"insurance"* off our to-do list. If you are creating a retirement plan, it's time to put insurance back on the list of priorities! Ask yourself, *"Do I have the appropriate amounts of the right types of insurance?"*

The study of consumer behaviour combines elements of economics, psychology, and sociology to look at who, what, when, where, why, and how we make the purchases we do. Theories abound for how people make decisions about everything, from where they go on vacation, to the type of car they buy, to the type of investment they choose. For simple issues, that could mean writing a list of pros and cons, flipping a coin, picking the cheapest option, or even cutting a deck of playing cards. With many decisions, the quality of that decision will come to light almost immediately. Was it a good vacation spot that we would recommend to others? Did the car perform as well as the industry reviews indicated? How are the investments faring?

The stakes are much higher when contemplating insurance alternatives. Whether the insurance product was right for your needs will only be proven in crisis, and at that point, there is nothing you can do to change the result. For that reason, insurance decisions are fraught with more anxiety than others.

One assumption about decision-making is that the players involved are rational. It can be challenging to think rationally about emotionally sensitive issues such as death, dying, illness, dependency, and incapacity. It demands making decisions based on *"what if"* when the *"what if"* is never a positive outcome. We are often prompted to re-evaluate our own insurance needs when someone in our peer group passes away or is struck with a debilitating medical problem. *"But she's my age!!!!"* That is when the *"what if"* materializes as a real threat and resonates with new meaning.

Insurance products and decisions are complex. The objective to safeguard the financial futures of yourself and your loved-ones provides powerful motivation to invest some time to assess your insurance needs and to seek qualified advice. Insurance is a product that is selected and purchased in the hope that it may never be needed. The key is that insurance should be bought, not sold. An insurance professional's role is to help identify the product or products that offset genuine risks. While the insurance professional is the best advisor for specific insurance companies and products, other professionals, such as your estate lawyer and financial advisor, can provide a second opinion or play a role in demonstrating how insurance can be a tool to eliminate some of the tricky or unresolved issues in your financial plan. Information and advice are readily available, so just start asking questions.

When I work with couples, I frequently observe that their insurance plan either consciously or unconsciously reflects their expectations in life. Men usually *"plan"* to die first – that is, they believe they will predecease their spouse. I never cease to be amazed, when asking that question in a course, by the level of agreement from the men and the stunned glances of their partners. Challenge your expectations - if the opposite occurred to what you expect, is your plan sound?

For singles, the decisions involve only one player. That can make wading through insurance choices easier when it comes to life insurance, but often more complicated for long-term care insurance and critical illness insurance, when there is no designated caregiver for support. We are either single (ever-single, separated or divorced) or potentially single (currently married or common-law). For potential singles, it means ensuring your insurance plan will still suit you as a surviving partner.

Too much insurance can be a waste of your money. Too little insurance or the wrong type of insurance may leave you exposed to risk. To achieve a risk-planned (not risk-free) retirement, finding the happy medium is a challenge best met by combining your needs with professional expertise.

E

Makiı

What Are N

Step 1 - Complete the ta
summarize your current in

Term Insurance				
Insured	Insurance Co	Death Benefit	Premium	Policy Termination Date

Group Insurance				
Insured	Insurance Co	Death Benefit	Premium	
SYF				

Whole Life Insurance				
Insured	Insurance Co	Death Benefit	Premium	Cash Surrender Value (CSV)

Universal Life Insurance				
Insured	Insurance Co	Death Benefit	Premium	Cash Surrender Value (CSV)

Critical Illness Insurance				
Insured	Insurance Co	Death Benefit	Premium	

Long-Term Care Insurance				
Insured	Insurance Co	Death Benefit	Premium	

...th an appropriate financial
...nsurance needs now and in
...ries in the adjacent table,
consider the following.

Do you need the insurance?

~ When you look at the coverage you have, will it be enough? Consider that term insurance and group insurance may not be there in the future. If you don't have enough coverage, consider putting the coverage into place before retirement.

~ Stop payments into universal life or whole life insurance and let the cash values in the policy pay for the cost of other types of insurance.

~ Keep the policies as needed, then cancel, surrender or terminate the plans at a later date to meet your changing needs.

If you don't need insurance . . .

~ Cancel term insurance first. If you do not need the universal life or whole life policies, you can cash them out for their surrender values. Watch for penalties and make sure you get a medical before you cancel. Do you really need the money?

~ Consider keeping the universal life and whole life policies even if you do not need them. They typically become more valuable the longer you own them. Also, the policies are likely worth more as a death benefit than the cash surrender value. As a result, see if your beneficiaries will pay for the premiums.

~ Even if you do not NEED the policies, you may want to keep them for their estate planning value to equalize an estate, ensure an inheritance or cover tax liabilities at death.

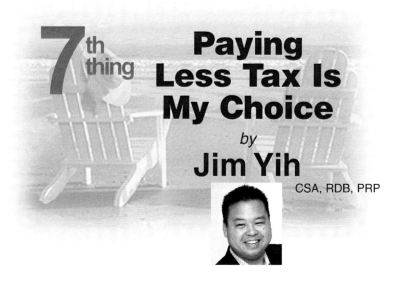

7th thing Paying Less Tax Is My Choice

by

Jim Yih

CSA, RDB, PRP

It has been said that there are only two certainties in life: death and taxes. At least with death it only happens once.

In my experience, there is a common perception that we pay too much tax and we would be better off paying less. The longstanding joke is tax is the only thing that brings the rich and the poor together on common ground – they all try to avoid paying for it.

Would you be happy if you paid no tax at all? Many would probably say, *"Yes!"* But paying little to no tax may mean that you also have little to no income. If you make more income, you are likely to have to pay more tax. Would you forego the income just to avoid paying tax? There is always a relationship between tax and income.

I remember one of the participants at a workshop complaining about taxes and how she should have never taken the bonus because she lost more than half of it to the Canada Revenue Agency (CRA). This is a great example of someone who does not understand the tax rate system. My advice is never, ever turn down money even if you have to pay tax on it! No matter what tax bracket you are in, you will always put money into your pocket.

There are many people who become fixated on the concept of not paying tax or paying as little tax as possible. The goal with tax planning should not only be about paying less tax but also about increasing personal net income as much as possible. Your net income is simply how much income you keep after paying the tax.

Paying tax is not necessarily a bad thing. For one thing, it pays for the many benefits we receive as Canadian citizens. In fact, paying tax also means you are making money and, the more money you make, the more money you will have even after paying the tax. Tax planning should be about **efficiency** - paying less tax without sacrificing income. Someone once told me,

> *"Taxation is the gentle art of picking the goose in such a way as to get the greatest amount of feathers with the least amount of squawking."*

So how do you do that?

In some respects, tax planning is very complex and can be incredibly intimidating to those who are not familiar with the rules and regulations. Anyone who believes that Canada's only two official languages are English and French has never read the Income Tax Act. In a book such as this it would be impossible to teach you everything you need to know about tax.

My goal is not to replicate the detailed tax planning covered in other books. My goal is to help you understand some overall taxation considerations and strategies so you can make better financial decisions through tax planning. Sometimes people get so focused on the little details of tax that they overlook the major factors. If you focus first on the overall picture, you might find that tax planning is easier - and more valuable - than you thought!

TAX PLANNING HAS A FAR GREATER IMPACT THAN INVESTMENT PLANNING

Imagine walking on a path until you reach a fork splitting the path into two directions. The sign at the first path shows 10 km to your destination. The sign at the second path shows 1 km to your destination. Both paths take you to the same destination but one is 10 times longer. Which path would you take? As long as this was not a trick question, most people would choose the shorter path. I share this with you because it highlights the difference between investment planning and tax planning.

A common perception is that the ticket to wealth is to make good investment decisions. I would agree that good investment decisions might help you make better rates of return - 1, 2, 3, 4 or 5% over time. Although good investment decisions will contribute to wealth, good tax planning can increase your financial benefit by 10, 20, 30 or 40%. If the path represents your road to retirement and the destination is financial freedom, then the 10-km path represents focusing all your efforts on making good investment decisions. Alternatively, the shorter path represents a focus on making good tax decisions to minimize tax. In other words, tax planning should not just be about maximizing the efficiency of your income but it should also be about maximizing your efficiency of effort.

If you want to plan for retirement, build more wealth, pay down your debts or improve your investment portfolio, start by understanding the basic tax system.

Tax Planning vs Tax Preparation

There is a big difference between tax preparation and tax planning. Every spring, Canadians start getting ready to file their income tax returns. It is at this time of year when we assemble our tax receipts to figure out how much we earned and how much tax we will have to pay as a result. It's tough to do any sort of strategic planning because everything has already happened.

Tax preparation, therefore, is really the act of summarizing the historical events of the past year. Tax planning, on the other hand, allows an individual to look into the future and try to develop both long-term and short-term strategies to minimize the tax bill.

So let's say at the first fork in the path, you took the tax path towards financial freedom because it would get you there faster. As you continue walking, you reach another fork forcing you to choose between two more paths. One path sign says Tax Preparation and the other sign says Tax Planning. Which path do you think would get you to financial freedom faster?

Tax planning will get you there faster because it gives you the ability to implement strategies in the future to reduce the amount of tax you pay and increase your net income. Unfortunately, this is the path least travelled. Instead, most people travel in life on the path of tax preparation by filing our returns each and every year and getting to our destination whenever we get there. Tax preparation is simply the act of filing a return, and the strategies needed to reduce tax are those that needed to be done far in advance. Tax preparation is something we all do because we have to. Tax planning, however, is something we should do to help us get to our destination of financial freedom faster.

Getting Tax Planning Advice

Many Canadians, in recognition of their limited understanding of the tax system, will utilize the services of professionals. I am a strong advocate of getting help and advice. Never assume, however, that tax planning will be given without asking.

For example, don't assume your tax preparer will automatically provide tax advice. Sometimes tax preparers aren't qualified to give planning advice. Even Chartered Accountants, who really understand tax planning, may not have time during the tax season to do effective planning with their clients because they may be so busy preparing returns and meeting the tax filing deadlines. Also, don't assume that the fee paid for tax preparation includes tax planning. Remember, the fee was probably for the time used to prepare the return. If you have someone who prepares your taxes for you, I would ask that person if he or she does any tax planning and whether you can set up a separate meeting to plan for the future. You might have to pay for the person's time but it may be worth paying for.

Your financial advisor may provide tax planning advice. Unfortunately, many financial advisors focus primarily on the investment portfolio and products because of the compensation arrangement in the financial services industry. That being said, there are also financial advisors in your community who will help with tax planning, but you have to ask for assistance in that area. If the relationship with your advisor has been primarily focused on investment, it may be worthwhile to ask if your advisor does tax planning or financial planning. If this is not his/her area of interest or expertise, then request referral to a qualified professional.

Learning More About Tax

So how can you learn more about **tax minimization**? One simple way to learn more is to complete your own tax return. Despite all the rules, remember that the tax system is designed so you can complete and file your own return without the help of a professional.

More and more people are taking the hands-off approach because it is much more convenient and manageable to have someone else do it. Today, tax preparation companies are profiting from Canadians by making tax preparation as easy as possible through software programs, on-line services and kiosks in multiple locations during tax season. The problem with making tax preparation easier is that it goes against one of the basic principles of good tax planning -- knowing the rules.

Getting someone to prepare and file your taxes may be convenient, but if you want to learn more about tax planning, it may be worthwhile to invest the time to do your own tax return <u>at least once</u>. Even if you get someone to prepare your returns for you, the process of doing your own returns is very educational. In addition to learning aspects of tax preparation, you will also learn to think about how you might minimize tax in the future. If you are working with someone who prepares and files your return, preparing the return on your own first can help you to start asking different, more specific questions, which in itself will improve your learning.

Tax minimization is the strategy of using tax measures in the Income Tax Act to reduce your tax bill. It is a smart form of tax planning that requires at least a basic level of knowledge. Don't confuse this with tax evasion, where an individual knowingly falsifies statements or fails to disclose income sources. Pleading ignorance is not well received by the government. The CRA takes the approach that you are guilty until you prove yourself innocent.

You can learn more about taxes by going to courses, reading books or talking to others. One of the best and simplest strategies for learning, however, is by doing your own tax return.

Knowing Your Tax Rate
You may have read or heard that 50% of your income goes to tax. Part of this belief comes from data provided by the Fraser Institute in its annual determination of Tax Freedom Day in Canada. Tax Freedom Day is the day in the year on which the average Canadian family has earned enough money to pay the taxes imposed on them by the three levels of Canadian government (federal, provincial and municipal). The taxes used to calculate Tax Freedom Day go far beyond just income tax. They include things like property tax, sales taxes, employment tax, fuel tax, tobacco tax and a host of other levies. Back in 2000, Tax Freedom Day occurred on June 24, which was the latest Tax Freedom Day recorded in history. That meant almost 50% of the money you made in the year 2000 went to some form of tax. The good news is taxes have been steadily declining since then. In 2009, Tax Freedom Day was reported to be June 6. The bad news is we are a long way from the earliest Tax Freedom Day, which was May 3, reported back in 1961.

Any way you slice it, we pay a lot of tax and a large part of it is income tax. Although income tax is significant, using a 50% figure is quite misleading. In our workshops, I am amazed at how few people really understand the income tax system in Canada.

Marginal Tax vs Average Tax

In Canada, we operate under a marginal tax rate system. In essence, the more money we make, the more tax we are privileged to pay. Marginal tax is simply the amount of tax paid on an additional dollar of income. As income rises, so does the tax rate. This is different from a flat tax rate where you pay the same rate of tax no matter your income level.

Knowing your marginal tax rate can help you make effective financial decisions. From a planning point of view it is not good enough to just know how much money you make. It is essential to understand how much you keep. Making a dollar doesn't allow you to count on spending that dollar. Knowing your marginal tax rate will tell you how much of that dollar you can utilize toward your lifestyle. If you are planning your finances or retirement, the focus should be on your net income.

In Canada we have two layers of income tax - federal and provincial. To illustrate how marginal tax rates work, my example shows tax rates for Alberta residents and encompasses **both provincial and federal tax**.

For the year 2009, there were four tax brackets:

$0 to $10,320	0%
(this is not really a bracket but the personal exemption level)	
$10,321 to $40,726	25%
$40,727 to $81,452	32%
$81,453 to $126,264	36%
over $126,264	39%

If you earned $50,000 in income in 2009, then you would be in the 32% marginal tax bracket and you would pay 32% of any additional dollar you made to the government. If you earned $100,000, then you would be in the 36% marginal tax bracket.

One of the biggest misconceptions about tax rates is that your entire income will be taxed at your marginal tax rate. Here's an example to show you how it actually works:

The person making $50,000 per year would not pay $16,000 in tax ($50,000 x 32%). Instead, his/her tax would be calculated like this:

$10,320 at 0%	= $0
($40,726 minus $10,321) at 25%	= $7,601.75
($50,000 minus $40,727) at 32%	= $2,967.36
Total tax	**= $10,569.11**

The marginal tax rate of 32% is the amount of tax paid on any additional dollar made up to the next tax bracket. In this example, the average tax is only 21.1% ($10,569.11 divided by $50,000 of total income). Average tax is the percentage of tax paid based on your total gross income and reflects the total tax you are paying. It is the total amount of tax you will pay through all the brackets divided by total income and will mathematically always be lower than the marginal tax rate.

The tax system varies from province to province. With 10 provinces and three territories, you can imagine the complexity of the Canadian tax system. Add in the fact that the rules can change every year because of provincial and federal budgets and you have an ever-changing and complex tax system.

If you have an interest in comparing the marginal tax rates for other provinces and territories, a table has been provided on page 199. The table includes marginal and average tax calculations based on an example of $50,000 and $100,000 of taxable income for the year.

THREE TAX STRATEGIES FOR RETIREMENT - DEDUCT, DEFER, DIVIDE

While the essential starting point for tax planning is the understanding of the marginal tax rate system, there are specific strategies that can help you organize your thinking on how to minimize your own tax in retirement.

When most Canadians retire, they will have the opportunity to lower and control their tax bill for a number of reasons:

~ They will have more control over their income in retirement,

~ If they have a partner, they will have more income splitting opportunities in retirement,

~ They will have access to tax credits that are geared especially towards retirees.

All tax strategies fall into one of three broad categories - deduct, defer or divide.

Deduct - A deduction is a claim to reduce your taxable income. It will reduce your tax bill by an equal amount to your marginal tax rate. Some common deductions include:

~ Pension plan contributions

~ RRSP contributions

~ Safety deposit box fees

~ Interest expenses

~ Union/professional dues

~ Alimony/maintenance payments

~ Employment expenses

~ Moving expenses

~ Professional fees

~ Child care expenses

Defer - A deferral strategy moves the obligation to pay current tax into future years. Deferring tax means you might eliminate the tax this year but you will eventually have to pay the tax down the road. Generally tax deferral has two advantages: (1) it is better to pay a dollar of tax tomorrow than it is to pay a dollar of tax today; and (2) tax deferral typically puts the control of when you have to pay the tax in your own hands instead of the hands of the CRA.

Income from registered pension plans, Canada Pension Plan (CPP), Registered Retirement Savings Plans (RRSPs), Registered Educational Savings Plans (RESPs) and various investment income strategies are the most common forms of tax deferral for the 'average' Canadian.

Divide - In one of my workshops someone said to me,

> *"It's not fair. I'm single and I do not have access to all the income splitting tax strategies that married couples can access."*

Unfortunately for her that statement was true, so maybe all these dating services have a new market to go after.

Income splitting is a very powerful tax strategy for those with a partner or other family members. The definition of a partner has broadened to include same sex, common-law and marriage-like relationships. Essentially, income splitting is the ability to split income with a partner or other family member who is in a lower tax bracket. For example, if you could have one person paying tax on $70,000 or two people paying tax on $35,000 each, wouldn't you rather have the second scenario?

Unfortunately, you cannot arbitrarily decide who is going to claim what amounts for income. There are, however, strategies to divide income within the rules set by the CRA including:

1. Using spousal RRSPs to help split income in retirement.
2. Sharing CPP retirement benefits with your spouse.
3. Splitting income from a registered pension plan.
4. Splitting income from an RRSP after age 65.
5. Investing the child tax benefit in your child's name.
6. Using RESP fund contributions.
7. Paying wages to family members (through a business).
8. Using partnerships or corporations to earn business income.
9. Using trusts.

This list is not exhaustive and may change with each budget. The ability to deduct, defer and divide may help you create a more efficient income in the future.

THE BIG PICTURE

Tax planning is a key component of financial success and yet it is still only one component of the larger picture of retirement. As I noted in the Investment Chapter, these ideas are like pieces of a puzzle. Do you know what the most important piece is in a jigsaw puzzle? The first piece? The corners? The edges? The last piece? Those are all important pieces but I would argue the most important piece in a jigsaw puzzle is the picture on the box. Can you imagine having a bunch of little pieces to the puzzle without ever having seen the final picture?

In the same way when you look at retirement planning, you have lots of little pieces. Tax is one piece. RRSPs, investments, lifestyle, spending, and assets would all be separate pieces. Each piece on its own doesn't make a lot of sense. It's not until some of the pieces fit together that the big picture comes together.

MY TWO CENTS

It's not always the details that count. Tax planning is easier than you might think. Knowing a few key things is more important than trying to memorize and understand the entire Income Tax Act. Make sure you grasp the importance of knowing your marginal tax rate and how to calculate your average tax rate. Having this skill alone will take you a long way in making good financial decisions.

The best tax planning is the planning that is done specifically for you. And more often than not, it will require some help from a professional or a team of professionals. Just make sure you find someone who can help you minimize tax as opposed to someone who will merely file your returns or invest your money.

Tax and the Telephone
Rein Selles

The caller on the phone was desperate. You could hear the stress in her voice by the speed at which her questions were asked.

"You have to help me. I don't have enough money to go out, to buy new clothes or even to replace my car. If I can't do those things, how am I supposed to save for retirement?"

Once she allowed me an opportunity to speak, I asked her to explain her current situation. It certainly sounded fine. She had a good job earning an above-average income. Contributions were going to a pension plan, which meant that some savings were already positioned for retirement. I asked her,

""I don't understand why you wouldn't have any money."

She replied, *"I just had to use all my savings.....that's why!"*

QUARTERLY INSTALLMENT PAYMENTS OF TAX
It is like waving a red flag in front of an angry bull. For most Canadians tax is silent and invisible. We take home our pay, net of tax, and may never look to see how much tax was paid. Retirees, however, are in a different position. While retirement income may have some tax withheld, it is often not enough to cover the full assessment. Income from a Registered Retirement Income Fund (RRIF) may only have minimum tax withheld. Some payments such as Canada Pension and Old Age Security allow an individual the choice of having tax withheld or not. I am sure that many retirees simply hope that by electing not to have tax withheld, the problem will go away.

When tax time comes, there may be two nasty surprises in store. First, there may be tax owing from the previous year. If those affected had spent their untaxed income without saving for the tax owing, there may not even be funds available to pay the tax. Second, a notice may appear from the Canada Revenue Agency requiring the retiree to pay next year's tax, in advance, by quarterly or monthly installments. This requirement occurs when personal tax outstanding on a tax return is more than $3000 for the current return and either of the two previous years.

Even those who give consideration to the amount of tax that should be withheld may have difficulty avoiding quarterly installments. For example, in the Canadian system there is no method of having tax withheld on investment income. Since the goal of retirement is to create income, many financial managers and brokers will move individual portfolios from growth (with capital gains deferred to a future date) to income - interest, dividends or capital gains. While some tax efficiency can be realized by selecting specific types of income from investments, there may still be some tax owing.

My next question to the caller was quite specific. Since her earned income from employment would have had tax withheld, the initiation of quarterly installments would have had to come about because of her investments. I asked her if she had non-registered savings.

"Oh yes. It is with a broker in Vancouver. He's doing such a good job too. I got my statement the other day and it keeps going up."

At this point you might well wonder why she doesn't draw on her investment account to buy her new clothes and car. Her approach, however, was to assign a specific purpose to different accounts. As a result, she wasn't seeing the connection between her investments, cash flow and tax. This often happens with those who receive inheritances or other windfalls. The funds are set aside, invested and then given a meaning where the owner is mentally prohibited from using the money. Unfortunately, the Canada Revenue Agency doesn't see it the same way.

The answer to her dilemma was quite simple. I asked her to make one phone call. That call was to be to her broker and should consist of four simple words, *"You pay my tax!"*

At that suggestion, she started to laugh. It took a few more minutes to explain the relationship of her outstanding tax and the income within her portfolio. Once she understood that the income should be used to help pay her tax, her view of the world changed.

It is never a problem to pay tax if you have earned the money to pay it. Pity the person who spends that money and forgets to save for the tax.

Tax "Myth" Information

Patricia French

Tax is one issue that, with a little explanation, does not seem as bad as originally expected. Of course tax planning is important, but many of us make a mountain out of a molehill. We often envision tax as something that steals our cake and leaves us with merely crumbs.

In teaching I find some of the best moments are spent demystifying taxes by dispelling tax myths and revealing the simple truths. Here are some of my favourites:

MYTH: "RRSPs are a waste of money...all you do is pay it all back in tax."
Jim's section on tax easily dismisses this tax myth. The belief that the cost is massive when we elect to withdraw savings from our RRSPs or RRIFs is passed on from previous generations. Our parents or grandparents likely expressed frustration at drawing on RRSP/RRIF savings either when they did not need the funds, but the rules mandated minimum withdrawals starting in their 70's, and/or when they did not plan and set aside (or have remitted by their institution) enough tax. *"April flowers bring May showers"* was the adage I grew up with. Retired generations came to believe April brought a storm of tax owing. They felt like they had to pay twice for every dollar of extra income...a little off the top at withdrawal and another chunk in April. An unexpected bill can get anyone down, but the impact was harder on those with limited incomes and savings. As with any unexpected expense, it can suddenly handcuff our lifestyle as we restrict spending until the bill is paid. It is quite easy to see how this could breed a bit of malcontent.

The truth is, no matter where you live in Canada, you keep more than you lose of additional income. Whether that is income from a part-time job, RRSP or RRIF, or investment income, your share is bigger. The tax withheld is based on some basic rules. For employment income, the rate of tax is calculated as though it were your only source of income. If you are already drawing pension income, there is a good chance your employer will not be taking off enough tax. For RRSPs and RRIFs, the tax withheld is based on the amount of the withdrawal and has nothing to do with your marginal tax bracket. The magic of knowing your marginal tax rate is being able to think *"net" rather than "gross"*. If your marginal tax rate is 36%, you know you get to keep 64% *"net"* and you need to have your employer or institution remit the 36% on your behalf or earmark it yourself for April. Money earned from employment and money withdrawn from RRSPs and RRIFs will easily conform to this simple math calculation. You need to keep a closer eye on non-registered investments as they can spit out sneaky annual tax receipts even when you have not withdrawn any funds.

MYTH: "RRSPs don't make sense if your pre-retirement and retirement incomes are in the same tax bracket."
This myth is based on an oversimplification of investment and tax. In a 36% tax bracket you would expect a refund of $360 on every $1000 contributed. The flip side is that you would pay $360 on every $1000 withdrawn. It sounds like you would come out even, so what is the point? The other thing to remember, especially as it pertains to investment income, is that you grew this money sheltered from tax. Your dollars, invested over time, worked with the market to increase in value. The result is far more potential income than you would have had if you elected to shove it all in your mattress to avoid the tax bill down the road. Even if you are in the same tax bracket pre- and post-retirement, you can win with an RRSP.

MYTH: "My pay increase put me in a higher tax bracket, so now I earn less than before."
This is a simple misunderstanding of Canada's progressive tax system wherein the more you earn the more opportunity you have to pay tax. The myth is that tumbling into the next marginal tax bracket will subject all your income to a higher tax rate. The truth is, income that spills over into the next bracket is taxed at the higher rate, and the rest remains unchanged. Enjoy every pay increase you receive without tax worries and remember that those higher paycheques will also help produce higher pension cheques in retirement if your pension plan uses a highest five-year average calculation.

MYTH: "We pay too much tax."
This myth is tricky because it harbours a grain of truth. This is not referring to any political critique of whether we should have to pay the

tax w[...] [Cana]dians do pay too
much [...] too much tax and
the Canada Revenue Agency [...] with personalized
suggestions to help us pay less. By adding our signature to our
income tax return we attest to being truthful and detailed as well as
that we understand. Understand the tax act...seriously? So, if we pay
too much tax it is like saying *"we meant to do that."* Paying too much
tax is usually the result of two problems: lack of knowledge or advice,
and poor planning or timing. And overcoming the first helps prevent
the second.

MYTH: "Tax is taking more and more of my hard-earned money!"

The cheery truth is the tax Canadians pay has been steadily declining.
This is a combination of better tax credits and tax deductions as well
as lower tax rates. Not only are the rates lower, but the jumps between
the rates from bracket to bracket are now more gradual. So, any
perceived disincentive to increase income is reduced. The difficulty for
retirement planning is that we cannot predict what the brackets will be
at or through retirement. To some degree, adjustments to plans have
to be made on the fly.

MYTH: "The annual contribution limit on TFSAs is too small to make any difference to my tax bill."

Tax-free savings accounts are still new to many investors. TFSAs,
announced in the 2008 Federal Budget and rolled out in January
2009, have given Canadians a new way to save where both investment
growth and withdrawals are tax-free. The word *"account"* is a bit of a
misnomer because it implies a TFSA is only a *"savings account"*; in
fact an investor can choose from a broad range of options including
mutual funds and stocks. While the program at introduction permitted
only $5000 per year of new contribution room, this amount will
increase over time indexed to the inflation rate.

If that still seems insignificant to you, consider two important points.
First, your TFSA has the opportunity to grow in value over time without
being taxed, giving it the potential to be a decent supplement to your
retirement lifestyle. And second, not only are withdrawals tax-free,
drawing from your TFSA does not impact *"income-tested"* benefits
such as Old Age Security and Guaranteed Income Supplement or
other tax credits such as the age amount for Canadians over age 65.
It can be a smart source of funds in a higher tax year, because it will
not add to your tax bill, and in a pinch could help you pay one.

Getting Start

With many thinç   ڊy way.
Most of us prefɛ   ovide a
straightforward :   ⁄ou can
learn the ins an   ɔur own
taxes and I enⲉ   owever,
understanding   ⁄ way to
get started witɦ

- ~ Plan ahead. In January, plot out your basic gross income for the upcoming year including employment income and pension income, as well as amounts you plan to withdraw from RRSPs or RRIFs. Plug it into an on-line Canadian Income Tax Estimator. There are several good ones that give you an estimate of your annual tax payable, after-tax income, and average and marginal tax rates. Now you have a better idea of whether enough tax is being deducted at source from employment and pension incomes, and the amount to ask your institution to hold back for tax on withdrawals from RRSPs or RRIFs.

- ~ Get familiar with on-line resources at the Canada Revenue Agency for access to forms and answers to common tax questions.

- ~ Keep good records. An organized filing system can save you and/or your tax advisor hours of stress and aggravation.

Making It Personal

Case Study on Tax

One of the most important skills you can learn is how to determine both your marginal tax rate as well as your average tax rate. Here's a case study to help you learn this important skill.

Rosie is 63. She is divorced and now just retired in Alberta. Her income comes from a few different sources: she has a pension giving her $18,000 per year of income, she is taking early CPP paying her $5,000 per year, she is working part-time making about $12,000 per year and she has some savings generating about $1,000 of interest income. Combined, her gross income totals $36,000.

1. What is her marginal tax rate?

2. What is her average tax rate?

3. If she wants to avoid paying tax at the end of the year, how much tax should she have deducted at source?

4. What is her net income (after tax)?

5. How much will she need to withdraw from RRSPs to get a net income of $32,000 per year?

See if you can do this yourself. If you get stuck and need help, the answers are on the next page.

See page 199 for provincial tax rates.

ANSWERS

1. What is her marginal tax rate?

   Rosie is in the 25% marginal tax rate since her total gross income falls between $10,321 to $40,726.

2. What is her average tax rate?

Income Range	Tax
$0 to $10,320	$0
$10,321 to $12,320 income tax credit)	$0 (due to the pension
$12,321 to $36,000	$5,919.75 ($36,000-$12,321 = $23,679 at 25%)

   Average Tax Rate

   ($5,919.75 / $35,000) X 100 = 16.4%

3. If she wants to avoid paying tax at the end of the year, how much tax should she have deducted at source?

   The answer is her average tax rate. She could request that each of the sources of income (pension, CPP, employer) deduct 16.4% in tax.

4. What is her net income (after tax)?

   $36,000 - $5,919.75 = $30,080.25 per year or $2,506.69 per month

5. How much will she need to withdraw from RRSPs to get a net income of $32,000 per year?

   To get $32,000 net income, she needs an additional $1,919.75 per year ($32,000 − $30,080.25).

   Since she is in a 25% marginal tax rate, she would need to draw $2,559.67 (gross) per year from RRSPs:

   $1,919.75 / (100% − 25%) = $2,559.67 (gross)

   $2,559.67 X (100% − 25%) = $1,919.75 (net)

   Calculating these answers is a great way to do some quick tax planning. Try answering these questions based on your personal income and compare it to your actual tax returns.

   Information on marginal tax rates for other provinces and territories is provided on page 199.

8th thing Planning Your Income in Retirement is Like a Treasure Hunt

by

Jim Yih

CSA, RDB, PRP

For most Canadians, retirement planning is all about having enough money. It's the one question that appears in every single workshop we do. The question of *"How much is enough?"* might take the form of how much money they need to save, how much income they need to maintain their lifestyle or how much time they should spend together! Since the ultimate decision to retire hinges on the answers to these questions, most people will want to quantify their retirement income.

In most cases, the answer to this question is simply a number. I recently saw a TV commercial from a U.S. bank suggesting that everyone had a different retirement number - $356,320, $1,623,020, $834,110 or $2,632,098. Their final pitch was to let the bank help you find your number. Although quantifying retirement as a 'number' is the mainstream approach to retirement planning, there are a few problems with that line of thinking:

1. **The 'number' is often intimidating** – When you factor inflation into the calculation, it can be hard to grasp that we, as individuals, may have to become multi-millionaires in order to retire. But it is no different than my father buying a starter home for $15,000 in 1965.

At that time, it would have been hard to imagine that same house would cost his kids over $100,000 30 years later. Or, that his grandkids would have to pay over $300,000 for their starter homes. Inflation can create disbelief in future numbers. If the numbers seem high, it can actually be de-motivating or discouraging. I remember working with a young motivated couple who had just gotten married. The bank did some projections for them and the outcome of the analysis was that they needed to have $2.7 million to retire at 55. To achieve this goal they needed to save over $2,000 per month. In their mind, something was wrong with these numbers because saving $2,000 per month was not feasible and yet they thought they were in pretty good financial shape before that meeting.

2. **The Capital Omissions** – Although having a specific number may be a reasonable way to look at the financial side of retirement planning, it does not account for the components of a retirement plan that do not translate into a block of capital or a number. For example, Canada Pension Plan (CPP) and Old Age Security (OAS) are two pay cheques you can receive from the Canadian government in retirement. These two sources of income are not expressed as a lump sum block of capital. When we consider CPP as part of our retirement plans we express the benefit as a monthly income not as an asset. We say, *"CPP is going to give me $600 per month"* as opposed to, *"My CPP is worth $150,000."* We may oversimplify wealth and retirement if we just look at it as a block of capital derived from the net worth statement.

3. **The Problem with Math** – Calculating your number is not as easy as you might think. Although the calculation is just math, there are a number of assumptions that can significantly affect the outcome. In fact, there was a bestselling book called *"The Number"* written by **Lee Eisenberg**. What is interesting about the book is that it focuses on the question and not the answer. Every number is based on a myriad of assumptions that will change many times over a lifetime. Are you using the correct assumptions?

4. **The focus on savings not spending** – Retirement income planning should be more about cash flow than a number. If you think about it, for our entire lives the foundation of financial security has been based on the process of making sure we have enough income to meet our expenses. Why would retirement be any different? One of the approaches to retirement income planning should be to look at it the way we look at financial security in our everyday lives - as a bank account with money going in and money going out. If you have enough retirement income to meet your retirement expenses then you should be ready for retirement.

THINK OF THE TASK AS A GAME

From my experience, when people retire without a retirement plan, they tend to adapt their lifestyle to their income. Since most people can see that they will have a lower income in retirement than when they were working, they start with the perception that they will have to cut back on their lifestyle in order to retire. The perception of cutting back in retirement goes against what retirement is supposed to stand for in the first place - financial freedom. Retirement is supposed to be the golden years, the best years of our lives. If you start with a mindset that you are going to have to cut back, is that a good foundation for building your golden years?

Moving from one employment pay cheque to multiple cheques from many sources in retirement can be a daunting task. Most Canadians receive their employment income electronically with tax already withheld, which makes spending and monitoring relatively simple. Retirees, on the other hand, are faced with the challenge that income may come from many sources, taxed at the minimum rate, if at all, and must to be applied for or arranged through financial institutions. It was all so much easier when we were working!

So, think of yourself on a treasure hunt. Where's my money? Try an approach to retirement income planning that makes the exercise fun.

SO HOW MUCH IS ENOUGH?

At the root of retirement income planning there are three steps to determining if you will have enough after-tax income to meet expenses:

Step 1: Plan Your Lifestyle

As outlined in Chapters 1 and 2, the starting point of a retirement plan is to think about what will make retirement the best years of your life.

Have you ever had moments where you were looking forward to something so much that you could not sleep? Maybe it was a trip, or a special course, or meeting an old friend. Whatever it was, it was so exciting that you could not wait for it to happen. Or have you ever experienced a day when time just flies by? Often time seems to fly by when you are having so much fun doing what you are doing that the activity just becomes effortless. Some people experience the opposite when the clock seems to be moving too slowly. This can happen when they are not engaged in what they are doing. They can't wait for it to end because it has little or no meaning to them.

Making retirement the best years of your life should be about replicating great moments. It should be about being so excited each and every day because you are doing the things you love to do. Ideally, these years of your life should be happy, fun and filled with meaningful activities that represent who you are and some of your passions in life. How can you know how much income you need or how much to save if you have no idea about what you are planning to do in retirement?

Step 2: Develop a Retirement Price Tag

Chapter 3 indicated the importance of understanding your spending in such a way that it would help you to recognize how much money you might need on a day-to-day, month-to-month or year-to-year basis. As I mentioned earlier, people will sacrifice their lifestyles to accommodate less income in retirement. Instead of adapting a lifestyle to an income, wouldn't the goal be to establish or create the income needed for the lifestyle you want?

Spending typically breaks down into one of two categories, basic expenditures and discretionary expenditures (pages 38 and 39). The price tag comes about when you can differentiate those expenditures that are essential to your survival from those that improve the quality of your life.

The closer you are to retirement the more important it will be to scrutinize your spending to determine your retirement price tag.

Check back to the Round Table discussion in Chapter 3 (page 43) where Patricia does a great job providing some strategies of how to better understand spending.

Step 3: Go Looking for the Income (Paycheques)

One of the key learning steps in our workshops is the hunt for income. The theory is that the more sources of income you have in retirement, the more money you will have in hand! Once you have a sense of the lifestyle you want and the price tag for your retirement based on that desired lifestyle, the next step is simply to begin the hunt for the paycheques.

THE EIGHT PAYCHEQUES OF RETIREMENT

For most of our lives, we go to work and earn a paycheque. What happens in retirement when we stop working? Where will our income come from? There are the eight possible paycheques a retiree could receive in retirement. Most people will get at least one of these paycheques and many will get more than one. The most financially secure retirees will get income from multiple sources.

1. **Pension Plans** – If you have a pension plan, you already have a head start at replacing some of your working income in retirement. About 40% of Canadians who are still working participate in a pension plan, and 56% of retirees collect a paycheque from a pension plan. For these people, pensions will form the foundation of their retirement income. The value of a pension lies in the fact that the saving was achieved by employee and employer contributions. In effect, the individual was saving twice as quickly for retirement. In contrast, those who are not in pension plans would need to save the capital using their Registered Retirement Savings Plan (RRSP) room or other non-registered savings. Either form of savings can be converted to a fixed income or pension at retirement. For example, a 65-year-old couple without pensions would need to save about $200,000 of their own capital in order to create a fixed income (or pension) of $1,000 per month.

2. **Canada Pension Plan** – This is one of two paycheques that will come from the government. The amount you get from CPP depends on how much and how often you put money into the Canada Pension Plan based on your employment earnings. For 2010, the maximum payment you can get from CPP is $934.17 a month, or $11,210.04 a year. These figures apply if you take the income beginning at age 65. You can, however, take CPP as early as age 60 at a reduced rate. Not everyone is eligible for the maximum. Canada Pension reports that the average monthly CPP payment at 65 was $501.32 (2009). The difference can be due to lower average career earnings, late entry into the workforce or reduced payments due to early retirement. If you are

interested in determining your own estimate of your CPP payments, call 1-800-277-9914 and press zero when prompted to talk to an operator. Canada Pension Plan is regularly reviewed and changed, if needed, to ensure that all Canadians can benefit at retirement.

3. **Old Age Security** – The second paycheque from the government is Old Age Security. It is a program that is funded out of general tax revenue. As a result, 99% of all retirees collect some amount of OAS. The benefit is based primarily on years of residency in Canada. Back in 1952, when OAS was started, it paid $40 a month, and payments began when the recipient reached age 70. (Incidentally, average life expectancy back then was 67.) In 2010, the maximum OAS payment is $516.96 a month, and recipients must be age 65 or older to collect. The average payment to a 65-year-old in 2009 was $498.53. There is no provision to take it any earlier than age 65. Other components of the OAS program include the Guaranteed Income Supplement and the Allowance for low-income earners. These supplementary benefits are affected by other sources of income and are recovered on the first dollar earned after Old Age Security is taken as income. For those who did not contribute to pension plans or CPP and arrive at retirement with no other income, the Guaranteed Income Supplement is an important element in providing Canadians with enough money for their basic lifestyles.

OAS Recovery (Clawback) – You may be aware that Old Age Security is subject to an annual income test based on Line 150 of your tax return. Line 150 includes all income before any adjustments. The test, conducted by the Canada Revenue Agency on each senior's tax return, measures the amount of gross income over a specific threshold. In 2010, the threshold will begin at $66,733 of personal income. When income exceeds the threshold, the government introduces a reduction in the Old Age Security payment that begins on July 1 and ends June 30 of the following year. In effect, the reduction is an additional tax (or surtax) equal to 15% of each dollar earned over the threshold and is withheld from the Old Age Security payment in 12 equal installments.

4. **Other Pensions** – Thousands of Canadians have pension funds on deposit with pension plans but have lost track of their contributions. This situation occurs when an employee terminates, leaves contributions on deposit and never approaches the plan for further information. In addition to pensions from a previous employer, you might have a potential pension at retirement if you were part of a military or police service, from an old insurance policy that provided annuity income at a specific age, survivor benefits from CPP if you survived your spouse, or foreign pension income if you worked and contributed to social security benefits in a different country for a qualified period of time. The bottom line is that no one is going to tell you about these forms of income unless you go looking. If your circumstances are uncertain, it may be worthwhile to dig a little.

5. **Employment Income** – A recent trend among older people is a return to work. Some retirees are starting their own businesses, consulting for their previous employers or working part-time. While those without pension income may work in retirement for the money, others work and earn income because they are bored or just want to keep busy. With studies showing that retirees today are more healthy and active than ever, it is not surprising that they would choose to work, if the opportunity presented itself. Economic pressures and social attitudes toward older workers prevented previous generations from re-employment. Today, working in retirement is very much accepted.

6. **Self-Employment Income** – There are two ways to work in retirement. You can work for yourself or you can work for someone else. There are some key differences between the two, which is why we break income from work into these two categories. There are two key benefits when you work for yourself - the ability to reduce tax on income earned in business, farm or rental by the legitimate expenses used to earn that income, and the freedom to engage in work at will. That freedom can be very nice but a concern with self-employment is that paycheques are difficult to plan. Alternately, while working for someone else may not

sound as glamorous, at least you know you will get paid for the work you do.

7. **Non-RRSP Investments** – You can create another source of income if you have investments outside of an RRSP. Such investments might include savings, bonds, stocks or investment property. Any asset that you own outside of RRSPs may fall into this category.

The income created from such investments might include interest, dividends and capital gains. Non-registered investments can be a good source of tax-efficient income since you don't have to pay tax on your original capital. Funds withdrawn from an RRSP are taxed as income as you draw them out.

Do not include your personal residences in this category unless you intend to create income by sharing space (i.e. room and board). You will always need a place to live, and to liquidate your house to supplement income is usually a last resort.

In 2009, the Government of Canada introduced Tax-Free Savings Accounts (TFSAs). The capital contributed to the account is already tax paid. The advantage to a retiree is that the income earned will never be taxed on withdrawal. It is important to note that, at the moment, TFSAs are not income vehicles. Rather, they are accounts where you would withdraw funds as needed and replace those funds in the account according to rules.

8. **Registered Retirement Savings Plans** – Unfortunately government programs do not provide enough benefits to support most people fully in retirement. If you do not have a pension plan, you may need to utilize RRSPs as one of the best ways to save for retirement. While you work, you reduce your immediate tax by the amount of the allowable contribution and defer that tax owing until the funds are withdrawn. The trick in the planning is to find the point in your life when funds withdrawn from an RRSP can be taxed at a lower rate. At that point, an RRSP provides a tremendous amount of flexibility. You can convert it to a Registered Retirement Income Fund (RRIF) or an annuity to

create a regular stream of income. The greater the value of your RRSP, the more potential income you will have at retirement.

KEY CONSIDERATIONS IN PLANNING YOUR INCOME

No matter where the income comes from, the goal for retirement income planning should be to have enough income or paycheques after tax to cover your retirement expenses (the price tag). Here are a number of key issues in planning your income that must be taken into consideration for an effective retirement plan:

Primary Income vs Secondary Income

Back in Chapter 3 (page 39), Rein introduced the concept of primary income versus secondary income. It's a good idea to take the eight paycheques of retirement and categorize them accordingly.

Remember that primary income has two characteristics. First, these cheques are paid for your lifetime and second, they have some provisions to deal with inflation. The sources of income that meet those two criteria are pensions, other pensions, CPP, and OAS.

Because pensions come first in planning, the last four types of paycheques become your secondary income. Unlike pensions, this income is not fixed and can be variable in nature. A major factor in designing secondary income is your awareness of the tax implications of receiving that income and the need to be directly involved in managing the process of creating it. For some, the necessity of involvement can become a very real obstacle to creating secondary income.

The Order of Paycheques

There is a logical order to payment in retirement that is reflected in the idea of primary and secondary income. Pension income, for example, is generally determined by age. Employment pensions can be paid as early as age 55 with some exceptions. CPP is next because you can access it as early as age 60. OAS comes into income at 65 (see illustration below). Finally, any remaining capital in an RRSP not yet withdrawn or paid must be converted to a minimum income as set out by the Canada Revenue Agency by the end of the year you turn 71. The flow of income creates a structure not unlike a set of steps.

When net income is measured against your basic and discretionary lifestyle goals, a very real gap may be visible that then determines the amount of secondary income needed.

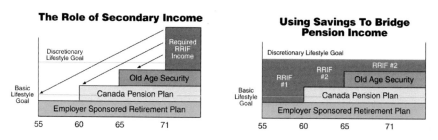

The Role of Secondary Income

Discretionary Lifestyle Goal
Required RRIF Income
Old Age Security
Basic Lifestyle Goal
Canada Pension Plan
Employer Sponsored Retirement Plan

55   60   65   71

Using Savings To Bridge Pension Income

Discretionary Lifestyle Goal
RRIF #1
RRIF #2
RRIF #2
Old Age Security
Basic Lifestyle Goal
Canada Pension Plan
Employer Sponsored Retirement Plan

55   60   65   71

As the second illustration shows, secondary income sources can be used to fill in the gaps. Traditionally the gaps were filled with sources of savings like RRSPs and other investment income or capital. Today, more and more people are filling in the gaps with income from employment. Remember, we still operate in a society where normal retirement occurs at 65. Why? Because that is the age when you qualify for all sources of primary income. If you choose to retire early, the absence of some pension income may mean that you will have more gaps to fill in and will require some savings or earnings to do so. In the end, if you have enough income to meet your expenses (both basic and discretionary), then you should theoretically be set for retirement.

RRSPs and Investments Are Used Last, not First

Often the focus of retirement planning is on having enough RRSP and investment capital. But how would you know how much income from an RRSP you might need without understanding what income your pension, CPP and OAS can create first?

For some people, like my father, the pension, CPP and OAS alone are enough income to cover expenses. In these cases, spending RRSPs can become difficult and can sometimes lead to *"grumpy retiree syndrome"*. Grumpy retiree syndrome happens with people who think RRSPs are a big scam because they are now at the age where they have to take money out of the RRSPs and pay the tax. Many are so bitter about paying tax that they avoid withdrawals at all costs so the government can't get its hands on their money. Then, at age 71, the government forces these retirees to take some of the money out and they get even grumpier because they have to pay the tax and sometimes at an even higher tax bracket. Avoiding grumpy retiree syndrome not only requires a good understanding of the marginal tax rate system in Canada (see Chapter 7), but also an understanding of other paycheques that you might receive in retirement.

Pre-65 vs Post-65 Income (Tax)

Once you turn 65, you will qualify for all sources of primary income - pensions, CPP and OAS. It is important in retirement income planning to consider how much income you will have after 65 and what marginal tax bracket you will be in. Doing so will help you to make smart decisions with your assets before 65 including:

- ~ Deciding whether it makes sense to draw RRSPs out at a lower tax bracket before age 65. Sometimes delaying RRSP withdrawal into the future can trigger OAS recovery (clawback).

- ~ Determining if there are opportunities to benefit from income splitting using spousal RRSPs, pension splitting or sharing CPP credits.

- ~ Deciding whether it makes sense to buy RRSPs at all. In some situations it may not make sense to buy RRSPs.

- ~ Determining if it makes sense to trigger capital gains before age 65 on investments or property that has accrued significantly in value. This may help minimize the potential for recovery on Old Age Security.

Spend for the Active Years

Back in Chapter 3, Rein talked about the three stages of retirement and how expenses tend to decrease the older you get. From a lifestyle perspective, it would make sense to use your money during the active years. If you have not used your money by the time you hit the stable lifestyle years, what makes you think you will use more of your money in your 70's, 80's and 90's?

Although this can make intuitive sense, it is not always easy to spend your money early in retirement because we all fear the possibility of running out. Money provides financial security and for many, the last thing they want to see is a depletion of their hard-earned assets even if it means forgoing rewarding lifestyle choices. This can especially be true for those who accumulate wealth because they were savers their entire life.

There is a strange psychological behaviour that happens with some people who have a great deal of money. They do not want to spend it because it represents a lifetime of hard work and their financial security. If you think about it, we are programmed to save. Then at retirement, we are supposed to switch our habits from being savers to spenders. But as the old saying goes, *"old habits are hard to break."* As a planner of your retirement income, it is important to evaluate your assets and develop a spending plan. For some, that will not be easy to do because we develop habits and values about dealing with money before retirement that are not necessarily appropriate after we retire.

Creating Income from Investments – In my experience as a financial advisor, most retirees fall into one of three categories:

1. **Savers** – The savers tend to avoid spending their investments even in retirement. They tend to live on their primary income (pensions, CPP and OAS). Savers would rather cut back on expenses than spend their hard-earned savings. They often believe that money provides security and it will be needed for a rainy day. Even though they have reached retirement, they still believe their money is best saved for the future and as a result, they often sacrifice their current lifestyle. Savers can find it difficult to spend capital in retirement.

2. **Preservers** – The preservers of retirement want to create income from their investments but they do not want to touch the capital. They are only willing to spend the growth or the interest, and emphasize how important it is to preserve capital. Psychologically, preservers recognize that wealth provides security so they do not want their wealth to decrease even if it means forgoing some current lifestyle expenditures. There is a balance in thinking with preservers because they are spending some money but still being fiscally prudent in preserving capital.

3. **Spenders** – The spenders in retirement are typically spenders before retirement and as a result, they do not have a lot of savings. They value current lifestyle and fear they will not get to enjoy their money before they die or become ill. Often you will hear spenders talk about how their retirement plan is to *"Die Broke!"* Spenders will often go into retirement with debt and even accumulate debt in retirement.

When you hit retirement, make sure your savings portfolio reflects that you have reached a different stage in life. If you are going to draw income from the portfolio, chances are you will need to make changes to the investments to generate income as securely as possible. Your need for income may outweigh your need for growth, accumulation and risk as discussed in Chapter 5.

If you are a saver, consider the importance of developing a spending plan with your investments. The alternative is that you run the risk of leaving too much in the estate, paying more tax than you would have when you were alive, giving it to your kids and having them spend it in ways that you would not approve of.

Don't Forget the Tax
Retirement income planning should never be done in pre-tax dollars because you can't spend your gross income. The only thing that matters is your net income (after tax). As we discussed in Chapter 7, it is important to recognize what paycheques you will receive in retirement and how much tax you will pay as a result. Proper planning means you not only need to know your marginal tax rate today but also your probable marginal tax rate in the future. Remember that withholding tax is not the tax rate you will actually pay. It is merely the amount of tax withheld at source until the final accounting is completed and the balance is due or a refund is paid.

IT'S ALL ABOUT A PLAN
When it comes to creating an overall income strategy, you need to pull all the pieces together to see the big picture. Retirement income planning is about:

~ Making sure you know where your income (paycheques) will come from,

~ Planning income in the right order, and

~ Creating enough income throughout the years after tax to cover your desired lifestyle (expenses).

Proper retirement income planning requires a plan. If you can't do it yourself, then seek help from a professional advisor who can help fit all the pieces together to develop the big picture for your retirement.

Learning to Turn On
(and Off) the Taps

Rein Selles

Have you ever turned on the water in a sink or tub, walked away and forgotten that the water is running? The outcome can be both embarrassing and very messy! The image that this situation creates is one that can also apply to planning your income in retirement.

Imagine that you have all those many sources of income generating a flow of dollars and then your attention is diverted from the income plan and you forget the money is still flowing. The account begins to develop a surplus cash flow and over a period of time, funds accumulate to a significant amount.

While having too much money in an operating account is not water overflowing the tub, I have had embarrassed looks from people who have five figure amounts in their saving or chequing accounts. While having cash on hand is not necessarily a bad thing, here are some issues to be aware of:

~ Income may have been generated from investment accounts on a systematic basis where units of mutual funds or stocks are being sold at market value. Sometimes this is taking place during a downturn in the market and can result in capital losses.

~ Converting an RRSP to an income stream will increase your taxable income. This is not an issue when the money comes out at a lower tax rate than in the future or if the funds are needed. The problem arises when there is no need for the money and your marginal tax rate increases.

~ Retirees may return to paid employment out of a need for increased social contact or purpose. While the employment income is likely welcome, it will come on top of all other income already in place and may attract more tax.

~ It is generally the case that funds accumulating in savings or chequing accounts have little, if any, investment return.

Having too much money seems like an odd problem to complain about in retirement. Why not just spend it? That could be an option IF the use of that capital does not affect the balance of the income plan over your lifetime. My own sense of surplus cash among older retirees is that it becomes a burden. Large balances are sometimes identified through bank or credit union reviews and depositors are invited to come in to discuss their options. Now, of course, you have to admit that you left the water running! Stupid money!

Imagine the amount of surplus cash as a *"fill to"* line on a tub, then you can understand that when cash exceeds that line, it is time to re-evaluate all the taps that are flowing and decide if some should be turned down or even off (if regulations permit). This is a simple and effective mechanism that you and your advisors can work toward.

In a retirement income plan, the steps include:

~ Determine your monthly cash flow requirement.

~ Create a tax-efficient and flexible flow in income from all eligible sources.

~ Include a surplus cash flow of $300 to $400 per month to offset annual irregular expenses during the year.

~ Evaluate at the end of the year how much surplus is in your account.

If the amount of the surplus is greater than planned ($3,600 to $4,800), have your income plan evaluated or increase your spending accordingly. If it is less, then you may need to increase your income or curtail expenses.

Year-over-year, the accumulation of smaller surpluses in an account like the Tax-Free Savings Account (TFSA) may allow you to take care of car replacement or capital repairs on a home - without affecting your income plan. A healthy surplus is what you plan for. Too much or too little shows the plan needs adjustment.

"Working" Your
Retirement Income

Patricia French

"Retirement: It's nice to get out of the rat race, but you have to learn to get along with less cheese."
~ GENE PERRET

For some pre-retirees the idea of juggling income in retirement from many sources is daunting. It can be trickier to balance cash flow when income is injected into the household throughout the month in dribs and drabs. One of the reasons people find they are not successful budgeting is that a budget is based on a month. For it to work seamlessly all income should be received at the start of the month and all expenses paid immediately afterward. Unfortunately, that's not how it works for most people. So planning around paycheques can not only streamline your cash management system, but can bolster confidence that you can reach the end of the month, before you reach the end of the money.

You may have noticed that little kids struggle to understand the value of money. Young kids will often choose *"more monies"* over *"one money,"* that is, prefer a handful of dimes over a $20 bill, because it seems like *"more."* It doesn't work the same with retirement income. While all those sources of income can add up to quite a <u>whole</u>, it may not feel like enough when you are only seeing the <u>parts</u>. Like a broken record, the warning is there will be *"less,"* and unlike the simplicity movement where *"less is more,"* the fear is retirement is where *"less is just ... well ... <u>less!</u>"*

The idea of several income sources may feel like a major change from your working years, but many of you will have been through this before. Was there a point where you held a couple of part-time jobs instead of one full-time position? In a dual-income household, did you have different pay schedules, i.e., where one was paid biweekly every second Friday and the other paid semi-monthly on the 15th and end of the month? Did you start a family and begin to receive family allowance or child tax benefits, usually around the 20th of the month? Very likely you have had some experience receiving multiple sources of income and you managed even during times when your financial demands were at their peak and money was stretched to the limit.

The most straightforward way to plan around your paycheques is to synchronize your expenses with your income. Imagine this as giving each income stream a specific work assignment, hence putting your income to work. You control when some sources of income are received *(i.e., investment income)* but not others *(i.e., work pension, CPP, OAS)*. You also have some control over when your expenses are paid. Ideally, your fixed money *(primary income)* will cover fixed expenses *(day-to-day expenses)* and your irregular income *(secondary income)* can cover irregular expenses *(vacations, renovations, celebrations)*.

To gain an appreciation for the schedule of your retirement income stream, a visual tool can lend a hand in *"proving"* how it will all come together. Start with an empty page from a monthly calendar. For the creatively inclined, consider using two colours of markers, one representing income and the other expenses. Begin with your income and note on the calendar the amounts of income you will receive on the days they will be received. If you would normally receive your work pension on the 27th of the month, write in *"Work Pension, $ Amount"* on the 27th in the calendar. In fact, most employer pension plan deposits will hit your bank account a couple of banking days before the end of the month and before Christmas in December. CPP and OAS payments arrive by direct deposit to your account on the third-last banking day of each month or arrive by mail during the last three business days of the month. December payments arrive about three business days before the 25th. Most retirees with pensions will receive the bulk of their income in time for the first of each month.

Continue until you have listed all your sources of income. Next, write in your expenses on the dates they are due. If you completed *Exercise 4* on creating a retirement budget, you can use those figures. Your dates do not have to be exact, because your objective is to get a glimpse of the big picture.

There are a few issues that meddle with methodical cash flow, not the least of which is part of our month can be acutely burdensome for expenses. Before the era of flexible payment options, the mortgage, arguably the single largest household expense, was usually due on the first of the month. With a couple of other significant expenses, the outlay in the first half of the month could exceed cash resources available. Great care would have to be taken to reserve income from the first half of the month so there would be enough to cover other costs. Look at your numbers to see if expenses put undue pressure on income during one part of the month. If the demands are not in balance with resources, you can manipulate the schedule. This could be as simple as breaking a key expense like a car or mortgage payment into more than one installment which can even out your month.

Consider paying when it makes sense. Remember many household expenses can be paid on a number of days (grace period), such as utilities, credit cards, and lines of credit. Pay expenses early if it is logical based on when you receive your income.

Watch for lulls in income in your calendar. Since most pension income will be available to you at the first of the month for major expenses, the knack is having enough to maintain your lifestyle through to the end of the month. You can avail yourself of your other sources of income to fill that gap. For some, supplemental income will be realized from investment and can be scheduled to be received mid-month. Even income from employment can play a role to smooth out the cash flow to ensure there aren't *"have"* and *"have not"* parts of the month.

For income that you choose when you draw, elect to take it with a direct purpose in mind. One of my clients lives on his pension incomes and only supplements his lifestyle using his investments on an annual basis for the family vacation with his children and grandchildren. This is just like assigning the receipt of an income tax refund to pay for bedding plants in the spring or an extra payment on the mortgage.

Create a fiscal cushion by building a small *"operating account"* surplus or float before you retire. The strategy of having a small surplus, equal to approximately one month's income, helps to regulate short-term discrepancies or fluctuations in income and expenses. It is a much cheaper alternative than bank account overdraft protection where fees and interest compound and consume your money. This is not to be confused with an emergency fund for sudden unforeseen expenses, as its purpose is to shield you from a serious financial mess. A surplus is a bright idea, but you can have too much of a good thing and leave too much cash sitting idly in an account earning next-to-nothing. Larger amounts of savings should be parked strategically in an effort to earn a return equal to or greater than inflation.

Leading up to your retirement, assess your retirement income and experiment with living at that level. It is a way to confirm if your intended retirement date is the right one for you. You may surprise yourself and discover you can retire sooner than planned. And while you may keep the same target date, how satisfying it would feel to realize you're only one bad day at work away from the option!

Exercise Ten

Making It Personal

Making Your Own Income Map

The structural model to map your retirement income is featured on page 148 and will allow you to "plot" the confirmed sources of retirement income that apply to you and to your family. The case study on pages 149 to 150 provides an example of how to complete the table.

Instructions

Begin the chart in the age column with the age of the first person in your family who will retire (you or your partner) and the other person's age that year. If you are both retiring at the same time, use your ages in the year your retirement will begin.

Starting with pension income, mark the appropriate box under the column with a small "X" in pencil when you expect a source of income to be paid or drawn. Once you have identified the sources of income that apply to you (and your partner), begin the process of gathering information on the amount of income, in today's dollars, that will be paid to you at retirement. Then fill in the appropriate columns and complete the chart by totalling the income sources and subtracting the taxes and expenses.

Researching Your Income

For employment pensions, contact your pension and benefits representative and request a monthly pension estimate for your planned retirement date and one logical date thereafter (so you can determine the value of working longer).

If you own a rental property, farm or sole proprietorship, estimate your average income monthly after deducting allowable expenses.

For Canada Pension Plan, you can determine the value of your monthly pension on your retirement date by calling 1-800-277-9914.

Information on current Old Age Security and Guaranteed Income Supplement rates and income testing thresholds can be located on-line by using a search engine and typing in "Old Age Security Rates."

Check with your financial advisor or broker for monthly income models based on the value of your registered savings.

To get an estimate of your investment income, check last year's tax return to determine the amount of income from non-registered savings by totaling the T3 and T5 slips that were filed (and divide by 12 to obtain your monthly income).

To get a reasonably accurate picture of your tax, use a previous year's tax preparation software (as if you were retired), visit a website that allows you to estimate tax on income, or talk to your financial advisor about having him or her do a projection using retirement income planning software.

RETIREMENT INCOME ASSESSMENT

Age at Retirement		Pension Income		Other Pensions		Canada Pension		Old Age Security		Earned Income		Other Earnings		Investment Income		RRSP or RRIF Inc.		Total Income		Less Tax		Net Income		Total Net Family	Withdrawal from TSFA		Less Lifestyle	Surplus (Shortfall)
You	Part.	You	Part.	You	Part.	You	Part.	You	Part.	You	Part.	You	Part.	You	Part.	You	Part.	You	Part.	You	Part.	You	Part.		You	Part.		

148

Case Study - The Johnsons

PAUL AND MARY JOHNSON

Paul (48) and Mary (46) Johnson are looking forward to retirement and want to determine how their sources of income will change. Paul's plan is to retire at 55 and then go back to work part-time until Mary retires. Mary works as a nurse part-time and plans to retire at age 60 with a small pension. Using Exercise 10, Paul and Mary have identified the following sources of income and expeditures in retirement with the assistance of their pension plan administrators, the Canada Pension Plan Call Centre (1-800-277-9914), the administrator of their RRSPs and an on-line tax calculator.

Paul

Employment Pension	$1,500 per month (unreduced)
Canada Pension Plan	$608 (reduced for early retirement)
Old Age Security	$516.96
RRSP	$50,000 (at 55) earning 2% annually
Savings	Held back as emergency funds

Mary

Employment Pension retirement)	$700 (reduced for early Canada Pension Plan
	$475 (reduced for early retirement)
Old Age Security	$516.96
Spousal & Personal RRSP annually	$50,000 (at 55) earning 2%
Savings	Held back as emergency funds

Lifestyle Expenses	$3,800 per month
Surplus Goal	$300-$400 per month to cover changes in cash flow from month to month
Inflation	Pensions are partially indexed to Consumer Price Index Canada Pension and OAS are fully indexed
Tax Considerations	Basic Exemption applied
	Pension Income Tax Credit applied
	Age Credit applied (after 65)

RETIREMENT INCOME ASSESSMENT - CASE STUDY

Age at Retirement		Pension Income		Other Pensions		Canada Pension		Old Age Security		Earned Income		Other Earnings		Investment Income		RRSP or RRIF Inc.		Total Income		Less Tax		Net Income		Total Net Family	Withdrawal from TFSA		Less Lifestyle	Surplus (Shortfall)
You	Part.	You	Part.	You	Part.	You	Part.	You	Part.	You	Part.	You	Part.	You	Part.	You	Part.	You	Part.	You	Part.	You	Part.		You	Part.		
55	53	1500								1000	2200							2500	2200	330	268	2170	1932	4102			3800	302
56	54	1500								1000	2200							2500	2200	330	268	2170	1932	4102			3800	302
57	55	1500								1000	2200							2500	2200	330	268	2170	1932	4102			3800	302
58	56	1500								1000	2200							2500	2200	330	268	2170	1932	4102			3800	302
59	57	1500								1000	2200							2500	2200	330	268	2170	1932	4102			3800	302
60	58	1500				608				600	2200							2708	2200	394	268	2314	1932	4245			3800	445
61	59	1500				608				600	2200							2708	2200	394	268	2314	1932	4245			3800	445
62	60	1500	700			608	475									800	800	2908	1975	449	207	2459	1768	4227			3800	427
63	61	1500	700			608	475									800	800	2908	1975	449	207	2459	1768	4227			3800	427
64	62	1500	700			608	475									800	800	2908	1975	449	207	2459	1768	4227			3800	427
65	63	1500	700			608	475	517								200	800	2825	1975	307	207	2518	1768	4286			3800	486
66	64	1500	700			608	475	517								200	800	2825	1975	307	207	2518	1768	4286			3800	486
67	65	1500	700			608	475	517	517							200	200	2825	1892	307	62	2518	1830	4348			3800	548
68	66	1500	700			608	475	517	517							200	200	2825	1892	307	62	2518	1830	4348			3800	548
69	67	1500	700			608	475	517	517							200	200	2825	1892	307	62	2518	1830	4348			3800	548
70	68	1500	700			608	475	517	517							200	200	2825	1892	307	62	2518	1830	4348			3800	548
71	69	1500	700			608	475	517	517							200	200	2825	1892	307	62	2518	1830	4348			3800	548
72	70	1500	700			608	475	517	517							200	200	2825	1892	307	62	2518	1830	4348			3800	548
73	71	1500	700			608	475	517	517							200	200	2825	1892	307	62	2518	1830	4348			3800	548
74	72	1500	700			608	475	517	517							200	200	2825	1892	307	30	2518	1692	4181			3800	380
75	73	1500	700			608	475	517	517							200	200	2825	1892	307	30	2518	1692	4181			3800	380
76	74	1500	700			608	475	517	517							200	200	2825	1892	307	30	2518	1692	4181			3800	380
77	75	1500	700			608	475	517	517							200	200	2825	1892	307	30	2518	1692	4181			3800	380
78	76	1500	700			608	475	517	517							200	200	2825	1892	307	30	2518	1692	4181			3800	380
79	77	1500	700			608	475	517	517							200	200	2825	1892	307	30	2518	1692	4181			3800	380

150

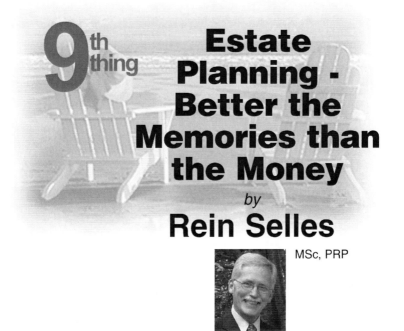

9th thing Estate Planning - Better the Memories than the Money

by

Rein Selles

MSc, PRP

"Your choices today allow you to leave your affairs at the end of your life as a lasting legacy. Either you will be remembered for how well you lived and ended your life or you will be remembered for how others had to untangle your affairs." ~ REIN SELLES

I t is a hard thing to do - thinking about one's own death. It is not hard at all, however, to think about how the death of others can make life difficult for the living. Some years ago I remember reading the results of a poll conducted by Royal Trust (now RBC Financial Group) on the role of executors or administrators of estates. The findings showed that the majority of those who had experienced the role of executor would never do it again!

This chapter will look at estate planning from the perspective of living legacies where the creation of good memories is a deliberate goal. In the Round Table, Jim and Patricia will follow up with suggestions on how estates can be organized more effectively for those who are asked to manage your affairs at death.

ESTATE PLANNING - WHOSE JOB IS IT?

When I first began teaching retirement I remember the presentation on estate planning as experiencing a slow death. The presenter, a representative of the Public Trustee's Office, talked at great length about the law and its implications. His point at the end of two hours (if you were still awake to grasp it) was that,

> *"If you don't make an estate plan, the government has made one for you and your heirs."*

That message, in and of itself, was a good one. What was missing, however, was any motivation to change behaviour.

Today, **Doris Bonora**, an Edmonton estate planner and lawyer, challenges her audiences in this way: *"Don't become a victim!"* That change in perspective puts the emphasis where it should be:

~ You have a responsibility to those who survive you to make your affairs as easy to administer as possible; and,

~ You have a responsibility to yourself to ensure that the lack of estate planning among those close to you does not place you in a position where you may have to sacrifice your own health and financial wellbeing on their behalf.

The first task is one you should approach with the assistance of a professional planner who is familiar with the law and experienced in estate planning. The second task is one that comes about through a more open form of family communication about life and death.

MOVING FROM DEATH PLANNING TO LIFE PLANNING

While estate planning presentations in the past tended to focus on what happens at death, more recent changes in legislation in Canada have created an interest in estate planning while one is alive. The range of planning extends as follows:

A   B   C

|-------------------------------------|-------------------------------------|

Alive (over 18)   Alive, but unable   Deceased
with legal rights   to exercise my rights   with a will to guide
                                                     my executor

152

~ An individual, who is over the age of 18 and not a dependent adult, is within his/her individual legal rights under Canadian law to make decisions (plans) and act on them (Point A).

~ There may come a time when you are alive but no longer in a position where you can legally make decisions with respect to either your personal or financial affairs. This may come about by accident and injury or by illness (such as Alzheimer's).

~ At death, all rights transfer to the province or territory under law. The goal of the will is to ensure that your wishes, rather than the obligations set forth in the law, are followed.

The law allows competent adults to set out directives, in advance, as to how they would like to arrange their affairs in the event of diminished capacity to act (Point B) or death (Point C). This is the unique nature of an estate plan. You have to be alive and within your rights (Point A) to create it!

ESTATE PLANNING AS PROCESS
Rather than seeing an estate plan as a single step (signing documents), it may be more helpful and interesting to see it as a process through life.

For Young Adults
Some young adults will argue that if the only thing you own is debt, why worry about having an estate plan? The problem is, you never know what you are worth until after you die. With life insurance through employment, life insured debt and death benefits from pensions and RRSPs, an individual may be worth more dead than alive!

For Young Families
Shared households, marriage and the arrival of children can create an increased awareness of the need for legal work to protect the family and ensure guardians and trustees for children in the event both parents are deceased. Those who experience marriage break-up and remarriage may have specific goals for the transmission of their estate that follow blood lines rather than rules set out under matrimonial law.

For Mature Families
As children mature, the role of executors may be repositioned to include those who stand to benefit directly from the estate. It is often at this point in family life when parents lend or gift funds to adult children for schooling, purchase of a home or start-up funds for a

business. While such gifting is done during one's lifetime, the implications may extend to the estate where children look back at all family transactions and ask, *"Was it fair and equal?"*

For Late Life Families

Concerns about caregiving and management of financial affairs give older adults motivation to look beyond the will to other legal documents including enduring powers of attorney and personal directives (living wills).

If estate planning can be seen as an on-going process of planning and action over a lifetime, our plans are more likely to serve us and our families effectively.

RETIREMENT AND ESTATE PLANNING - IRRECONCILABLE DIFFERENCES?

If I contrast two current points of view in popular literature about estate planning and retirement, you can see the problem:

> *"Die Broke"* by **Stephen Pollen**, and

> *"Don't Die Broke*: How to Guarantee Your Income for Life and Keep Your Retirement from Going Belly-Up" by **David J. Reindel.**

The goal of *"dying broke"* resonates for many of today's retirees particularly because so much intergenerational support has already taken place. For parents who have paid for their children's education and facilitated child launching with their own funds, the idea of leaving an estate may seem like an irrational act.

A quick exercise often clarifies the family side of estate planning:

> *Take the number 85 and subtract the age you were when you had your first child.*

The resulting number is the possible age at which your child(ren) would benefit from the estate. The question becomes, *"Does a child who is 55, 60, 65 or even 70, need to benefit from an estate?"* In some families and cultures, the answer would still be *"Yes!"* because the goal is to leave each generation more enriched than the last. If the answer is *"No,"* then there could be a direct relationship between your lifestyle in retirement and the value of the estate after death. The difficulty is that in the absence of an exact date of death, planning to die broke becomes a risk not a goal.

Here are some specific guidelines that may help organize your thoughts:

~ If you are fortunate enough to be able to live in your home through your lifetime, the value of your property will form part of your estate. Some will argue that a move into a care facility will deplete the capital gained (tax free) from the sale of a principal residence. I would argue the greater risk is that the capital will still be in the bank - with interest!

~ Whether you are a connoisseur of fine art or a collector of rare stamps, art and collections will accumulate in number and value as your interest and budget allows. Add time to the mix and a collection you would never part with while you are alive can become a nice surprise for relatives after your death.

~ The death benefit from an old insurance policy could increase the value of your estate tax free.

~ Lastly, capital can accumulate inadvertently when your lifestyle changes with age. The surplus cash generated by the lack of spending can create an emotional response that begins to assign a human characteristic to an inanimate object - **stupid money**! More surplus cash may also mean more investment income and, as a result, more tax every year. Family members will recognize the problem when parents begin to complain about the necessity of dealing with quarterly tax installments. Such installments come about primarily because tax cannot be withheld on investment income. Many older adults who begin to accumulate non-registered investment capital will find the physical act of having to write a cheque quarterly to Revenue Canada a frustrating and painful experience.

Living Legacies

Edmonton estate planner **Ron Knol** addressed the issue of the estate by issuing a unique challenge to his audiences: *"Would you rather give with a cold hand or a warm one?"* His challenge forces you to consider whether an estate plan is one that deals with assets at death or one that allows the living to create a lasting memory with money gifted or used in a lifetime.

I have had the privilege of coaching many families around *"living legacies."* The process I use generally follows this pattern:

~ What are the requirements for guaranteeing sufficient income over the family's lifetime (see also Chapter 8)

~ What amount of capital should be set aside so that the family can access cash when needed? This could also include benefits while living from an insurance policy (such as long-term care insurance).

~ What is the value of assets remaining (including the principal residence)?

~ Does life insurance increase that value at death?

~ Is that enough of an estate?

When the answer to the last question is, *"Oh, that's too much!,"* a discussion on living legacies can begin in earnest.

What Is a Legacy?

A few years ago, at the request of a study group of professional planners, I did research on the meaning and use of legacies. A good definition of a legacy was one given by Edmonton solicitor, **Lyndon Thiessen**.

> *"(A legacy) is something separate from who we are - that stands in its own right and that, when created, reflects one or more values of the person and can survive beyond the person's lifetime."*

Lyndon's definition points to a critical element in the planning of a legacy - the recognition of the importance of personal or family held values in decision making. Would you be able to recognize the values that form the basis of your personal plans? The exercise at the end of this chapter will help you list and prioritize your values.

What Is the Purpose?

Neil Fenna, another member of the study group, put the purpose of a legacy in this way,

> *"...to create a lasting, positive impression associated with your name that would leave the world a richer place."*

What Kinds of Legacies Are There?

Using interviews with a variety of professional planners, I identified some of the following types of legacies:

Passion or Community Legacies

These legacies are built around a cause you believe in or by building community support for a common need. An example might be a parent of a special needs child who fights to ensure the right of her child and others to education and care.

Reflective Legacies/Personal Histories

Sometimes a legacy is simply to have your life remembered. I try to encourage older adults to write their personal story (or dictate it), so that members of the family and community can draw on that knowledge. Living history projects have been sponsored by some school boards and bring retirees and school children together to share stories. In addition to generating stronger understanding between generations, children hear of occupations and experiences that make history come alive. Jim has developed a new tool to help people organize, diarize and share their life legacy and stories with the people they love. For more information, see page 164.

Business Legacies

While many business ventures are sold outright, some owners will develop their business so either their children or employees can take over. The business itself then stands as the legacy. In St. Albert, the Holes Greenhouse operation is an excellent example of a business legacy within a family.

Leadership Legacies

There are those who, by their name and example, can instill in others motivation to support a cause. Good examples are the Nelson Mandela Children's Foundation or the Aga Khan Foundation.

Financial Property/Charitable Gifts

Many organizations and charities benefit by receiving the transfer of wealth or property via a will or through gifts while the individual is alive. Because charitable gifts have implications for taxation, many charities have developed extensive support to assist families and individuals in planning charitable gifts at death.

Territorial or Physical Legacies

These legacies come about in response to the question, *"What places have made a difference in your life?"* Because of your emotional investment in a place, you may feel it is important to create a physical legacy. The creation of Pier 21 Museum in Halifax is a good example of a physical legacy for some of the immigrants to Canada who came through the immigration centre between 1928 and 1971.

Gifts of Life

This refers to the decision to donate an organ or body part so that another person may have an opportunity to live. The simple act of completing the required documentation on your driver's license or health care card could make all the difference to someone who is waiting for an organ transplant.

Life Balance Evaluation

This is an exercise that helps identify events that have shaped an individual's life and focuses on the strengths and knowledge created from those experiences. Using a 8.5" X 11" sheet of paper, the page is marked with a vertical line showing a scale from -10 to +10 (where zero is the centre of the page) and a horizontal line showing age beginning at 18.

I ask participants to begin with the high point of their lives (i.e. graduation, marriage, birth of a child, etc.) and, using the positive side of the scale, where that event would be placed as a score (0 to10). Next, I ask for the lowest point of their lives (i.e. an illness, divorce, loss of a job, etc.) and the score on that event on the negative scale (0 to -10). With two reference points, individuals can review other life events and mark them on the chart. The final step is to connect the dots. The life line provides an image of how life has moved forward both positively and negatively.

Gifts of Joyful Memories

The goal of this type of gift is to create a shared memory with those you love. For example, an 80-year old widow took all of her children and grandchildren on a cruise to Alaska. She could have equally stayed home and left the money to her family at death. Which course of action would have been more joyful?

In my interview with a parish pastor, he told me the story of his grandmother's gift on birthdays. Each year, his grandmother would send a two dollar bill enclosed in a card to each family member. After her death, the family discovered a stack of two dollar bills ready to be mailed out at the appropriate time. As a testament of her thoughtfulness, a two dollar bill was framed and given to each family member in joyful memory of their grandmother.

Getting Organized to Plan a Legacy

Based on the common mistakes identified by professionals in the field, here is a list of key strategies that will help you create your own living legacy:

- Live your life in a way that creates a legacy.

- Focus your plans on what you can accomplish by living rather than what you can achieve in death.

- Obtain and act on professional advice.

- Recognize that a legacy may involve formal structures to be successful.

- Be passionate about your beliefs and values.

- Don't let tax become the sole purpose of your legacy. The real value lies in how it will benefit others.

- Be clear in your objectives and share them with others.

Organizing Your Estate

Jim Yih

The quote Rein uses at the beginning of this chapter about how you might be remembered, really highlights the importance of having a well organized estate plan.

In my discussion, I would like to look at estate planning from a really practical perspective - the perspective of the executor. This person will be the one who has to deal with your affairs after your death.

THE EXECUTOR

Who have you chosen to be your executor? Chances are, you have chosen someone close to you that you think is capable of handling the job. More often than not, an executor is someone in the family. The problem is, just like the poll by RBC suggests, you may be placing a significant burden or problem upon someone you love if you have not taken time to think this through properly. So maybe the solution is, instead of making someone we love the executor, we should give the job to someone we hate! Obviously, that's not the right alternative.

I don't think people take enough time to really think about the role of the executor and what is required and how they can make that role easier. For me, estate planning is all about making sure relationships are preserved and letting the people you love focus on what matters the most - your shared memories and your legacy

HOW DO YOU CHOOSE AN EXECUTOR?

The executor is the legal representative of your estate appointed through a will. If you do not have a will, you have not appointed anyone to be in charge when you die. The executor is the person in charge of the estate, in the same way a CEO is in charge of a business. He or she will have to make funeral arrangements, take stock of what is in the estate, pay all expenses and debts, prepare and file tax returns and eventually disperse the estate according to the instructions in the will. As you can see, executors can have a lot on their plate and if you add in any level of complexity, like a business, foreign assets, multiple properties, families that do not get along or, worst of all, dealing with the estate of a hoarder - someone who keeps everything and throws nothing away, settling an estate can be a lot of work and take a long time.

You can have more than one executor if you wish. In fact, it is always good to appoint a back-up or alternate executor. The ideal executor can make a big difference in estate settlement. Here are some characteristics of the ideal executor:

~ Is someone you trust,

~ Lives in the same area as you,

~ Has experience managing money and dealing with financial institutions,

~ Can deal with your relatives and beneficiaries objectively,

~ Is comfortable dealing with lawyers and accountants,

~ Has the time to spend settling your estate, which is a part-time job for one and a half to two years,

~ Has the patience to deal with government agencies (especially tax departments),

~ Is organized and willing to do lots of paperwork,

~ Is not afraid to ask for professional help when needed,

~ Has experience settling estates or is willing to read, research and learn,

~ Is likely to outlive you.

The executor is likely to be someone you care about and most certainly will have to deal with others you care about.

MAKING LIFE EASIER FOR THE PEOPLE YOU LOVE, ESPECIALLY YOUR EXECUTOR

There is no question that estate planning really involves three essential legal documents: the will, enduring power of attorney (EPA) and personal directive. The terminology may change depending on where you live in Canada. The intent of each document, however, is the same. These three documents form the formal written part of an estate plan. All other estate planning decisions, such as beneficiary designations and how you distribute certain assets, must work in concert with these three legal documents.

Making life easier for the people you love not only requires the formal or legal part of estate planning but also three key components of estate planning: organization, diarization and communication.

GET YOUR ESTATE ORGANIZED

When somebody dies, typically a lot of questions come up. Where do you find a copy of the will? Who is the financial advisor? How many financial advisors are there? How many bank accounts are there? What were the wishes for a funeral service? Who needs to be contacted? Where are the investment statements? Unfortunately, the one person with all the answers has died. Having an organized estate will not only help you feel better about your personal finances but it will also help the people you love who must make decisions at an emotionally difficult time.

Can you imagine your executor or beneficiaries coming into your house today and trying to find documents, statements and files in an effort to try and come up with answers to important questions? If you don't have your financial documents organized, it could take days, weeks, months or even years to sort through everything. How long would it take you to get organized? Probably a tenth of the time it would take someone else to do it.

Getting organized is all about gathering information so you can answer all the questions while you are still around to do so. When it comes to estate planning, many people don't know what information to gather and what questions will be asked when they die. Here is a general guideline of some of the information you need to put together to get organized for estate planning:

~ **Legal documents and a list of financial assets**. Obviously you will need the will, and the enduring power of attorney and the personal directives if the individual has no legal capacity (as defined by the documents). You will also need account and policy numbers on all financial accounts like bank accounts, mortgages, property information, investment accounts, RRSPs, insurance policies, credit card accounts, etc.

~ **A list of key financial contacts.** It would be helpful for the executor to know who to call including your lawyer, financial advisor(s), the institutions you bank at, insurance agents, human resource people at work, etc.

~ **A list of key personal contacts.** Your family may not know people like your friends, co-workers, doctors, people from your past jobs, etc. There are obvious people who will be notified when someone dies but there are often layers of people who get missed because the family has no idea of whom to call beyond the obvious. I remember that I did not know very well many of the visitors at my mother's funeral but I appreciated that they took time to pay their respects. I am thankful they saw the obituary notice published in the newspaper.

~ **Funeral information.** Since, in many instances the funeral happens before the will is read, it is important to let your executor and beneficiaries know what you want for funeral plans. If you have made pre-paid arrangements, let them know where you have made these arrangements and give them a copy of the supporting documentation. If you have a special song, flower, poem or charity, it would be nice to include that information with your documents because they will feel good about incorporating your wishes into the ceremony.

~ **A list of important personal belongings.** You may also need a list of any of your specific assets that you want to give to specific people. Often a will provides general direction for major assets but if you have meaningful heirlooms that you want to give to specific people, a list of such personal items and the intended recipients is very helpful because these items typically can't be split. Money can be split evenly but items like mom's wedding ring, the family painting or dad's office desk cannot. Whatever the heirloom, it can often be a source of family conflict. Remember the will gives general direction but not usually for distribution of specific belongings.

~ **A list of passwords.** In the new Internet era, it may be helpful for your loved ones to have the passwords for on-line access to various things like your investment accounts, bank accounts and even social network sites like Facebook.

Once you've gathered the information, you now need to diarize it. The information needs to be put on paper or in an electronic document, if you also provide the password. The document could be stored in a file cabinet or a binder or a specific place in the home office.

The last important step, which is the hardest, is to **communicate the plan.** Why is this step so hard for so many people? Sometimes there is a perceived social taboo when it comes to talking about death and money. Death is a reality and we would be far better off if we opened up the lines of communication between generations and talked more openly about the relationship of death and money.

USING TOOLS

As a result of seeing so much disorganization and conflict when someone dies, I have developed a new software program called **My Estate Organizer** to help people organize, diarize and share their estate affairs with the people who most need the information.

My Estate Organizer is a software program that asks you to answer a series of questions that will provide answers for your executor, beneficiaries and family when you pass away. Completing **My Estate Organizer** is the gift of love that will provide peace of mind for your executor and beneficiaries. You will save them hours, days and months of work, headache and stress.

I know some executors who have made completion of the questions in My Estate Organizer mandatory before agreeing to become an executor. As your affairs change it is also helpful to have a tool that is easy to adjust as needed.

To learn more about how **My Estate Organizer** can help you start the process of estate planning, visit the website **www.MyEstateOrganizer.com.**

Last Love Letter

Patricia French

We tend to think of our **estate** as our wealth that we want to distribute and an **estate plan** as the chronicle of what will be done to disperse that wealth. In reality, both the estate and the estate plan are the tangible expression and sharing of your lifetime accumulation of wisdom, fortitude, relationships, values, intentions, resources, and possessions. It's not just the *"stuff."*

"What you leave behind is not what is engraved in stone monuments, but what is woven into the lives of others." ~ PERICLES

While we might prefer that it were not so, money can often represent relationships and values. Relationships are very sensitive in the area of financial issues. Couples argue about money, parents may come into conflict with each other and their children over allowance and financial assistance, and loans exchanged privately between family members make front page news at holiday gatherings. A well designed estate plan is a way of expressing your feelings, not only in how you elect to distribute all that you have accumulated, but also in your concern to ease the burden of decisions at a difficult time for your loved ones. To frame the process positively, think of it as writing one **last love letter** to your family, friends, and community.

As a young child, I remember my maternal grandparents coming to visit from Manitoba. Each trip there would be a serious discussion between my parents and grandparents after dinner one evening, and my brother and I would be given the opportunity to escape from the adult conversation. My grandfather worked in the insurance industry for decades and took estate planning very seriously. While it was a great relief to get to avoid that annual meeting as a child, as an adult I have come to admire how my grandparents valued open communication about their plans. To me it was the ultimate gift for our family to know what to do *"in the event of."* I'm not sure how they overcame the hurdle of discomfort that comes with discussing their own incapacity and death, but they did. Having aging family members living at a distance creates challenges when their needs increase, and yet an open dialogue allowed my parents greater peace of mind.

From laughter to anger to tears, people experience the gamut of emotions when they begin to prepare an estate plan, not the least of which may be a feeling of incompetence about the task ahead. There are many good books and tools to help guide you through the process, but it can be helpful to examine how you might feel when writing down your final wishes. This is the first obstacle - the acceptance that there comes a point when you won't need your personal property anymore.

One model of learning draws on a four-stage process which leads to becoming competent in knowledge or skill. The first stage, **Unconscious Incompetence**, is characterized by *"you don't know how much you don't know."* This is where we typically find ourselves when we first grasp that we need to devise an appropriate estate plan but understand little about the process. At this stage it is not uncommon to have the sense that this won't be too hard. We may believe the biggest challenge is having a stiff upper lip, and coming to terms with the idea of planning around death. Expect to ride waves of emotions as you reflect on your life and your loved ones.

In the next stage we dive into information gathering and begin to take in as much as we can about estate planning. We read books and articles, poll our friends and relatives, and perhaps attend educational seminars. At this time the feeling can be "information overload". This stage is referred to as **Conscious Incompetence** and can be thought of as *"you know how much you don't know."* The scope of the undertaking can feel overwhelming and there may be more questions than answers. We quickly gain an appreciation of the significance of designing the plan. Frustration can set in and you may want to push it all aside. This is a time to get professional advice to keep on target.

Families can be complicated and we may not have enough answers. It is in our hearts to treat our kids equally, but the reality is children from the same family can have different needs and may require different levels of support, during and following our lifetime. A child may have had more difficulty getting launched or have experienced financial setbacks that required parental intervention. You may foresee that a child will need extra help in the years ahead. You may want to recognize a child who played a larger caregiving role in your later years or made a greater contribution to a family business or farm. Like it or not, siblings may be keeping score.

> *"Mom and dad gave Jimmy the down payment on that house, just because he couldn't get it together to save his own money...I did it myself, why should I be punished?"*
> *"Joe should get the farm, he's been doing all the work around here, and besides, the other kids moved to the city."*

Your plan can match the needs of your family. You may feel obliged to balance the score. If one child received money from you for a major expense, you could make allowance to even things up in your will. You may want to acknowledge the special sacrifice of a child in assisting you at home or with business interests. You may also want to forgive debts. Your best plan is to aim for fair, not equal.

Think about an example of a family cottage. In an effort to treat children equally the cottage could be left to all the kids. That would be equal, but is it fair? If only one kid lives close enough to use the cottage, is it unfair to children who live a distance away? An alternative would be to leave the cottage to the child who would use it, and give investments of equal value to the other kids. That solution isn't perfect either. Now, one kid has a property that carries with it a potential sentimental burden. There could be family fallout if the child ultimately decided to sell the *"family cottage"* and with it all of the memories, whereas not a word would be said if the siblings spent the savings. There is no doubt that the decisions are fraught with apprehension and uncertainty.

Getting professional advice is the second barrier that brings estate planning to a standstill. We may have the best of intentions to get our estate plan defined on paper, but we hesitate to book the appointment. Some claim it is the expense of the expertise that is the deterrent, but I believe it is a worry much greater than the dollars. I think we presume we need it all figured out before we attend the meeting, and that all a lawyer does is write our wishes in *"legalese"*. An experienced estate planner or lawyer can suggest solutions to some of the most complicated and delicate dilemmas and can be an objective source of reason.

Conscious Competence is the third stage in learning. The *"you know how much you know"* period is where you can see your estate plan is beginning to come together. Knowledge and skill have merged and you begin to invent your own solutions and feel capable, though you need purpose and dogged determination to apply that which you have just learned.

Finally, you arrive at the final stage of **Unconscious Competence** where *"you don't know how much you know - it comes easily."* Your confidence is high, your feelings clear, and you plan with ease. Backed with knowledge, skill, and professional advice, you are competent to create the legacy that endures beyond your lifetime. This is a good stage to share your plans with your nearest and dearest.

Open the lines of communication with your family about your wishes. Talk to your kids about their requests and expectations. You may be surprised to learn which family heirloom is most significant. One of the most meaningful gifts I received from my grandmother is her box of recipes. It's not always about the money but the memories. Written in her handwriting, the recipes bring back fond memories of baking cookies and pulling taffy.

Your decisions are yours and yours alone. You hope though that the decisions you make will be understood by your family. Since money and relationships are inextricably intertwined, it is vital to realize that the decisions you make can reverberate long after you are gone within the relationships of those left behind. If your family does not agree with how you determined to divide your estate, their frustration with your choices can manifest as a wedge that distances and challenges their relationships.

The best approach is to talk about your decisions with your family. This will allow your family to address any concerns with you directly and it need not become an issue that wounds family relationships in the future. I will not minimize the emotional challenge of starting those conversations, except to say, as hard as it is, do it anyway. Through understanding, your **last love letter** can serve to nurture and protect those relationships, rather than put them at risk.

Exercise Eleven

Making It Personal

Values Exercise - Step One

Using the list below, cross out those values that are not important to you until only eight or less remain. Feel free to add values that may not be in the list.

_____	Achievement	____9____	Security
_____	Adventure	_____	Service
_____	Aesthetics	_____	Simplicity
_____	Affiliation	_____	Spirituality
_____	Altruism	_____	Stability
_____	Challenge	_____	Status
_____	Competence	_____	Structure
_____	Competition	_____	Time Alone
_____	Contact with others	_____	Tranquillity
_____	Creativity	_____	Variety
_____	Excitement		
_____	Family	____5____	WILDERNT§
_____	Fast Pace	____7____	ACTIVET
_____	Friendships		TRAVEL
_____	Health	_____	_____
_____	Helping Others	_____	_____
_____	Independence	_____	_____
_____	Influence	_____	_____
_____	Integrity	_____	_____
_____	Learning	_____	_____
_____	Legacy	_____	_____
_____	Material Gain	_____	_____
_____	Productivity	_____	_____
_____	Respect		
_____	Risk		

Step 2: Use the area below to select and prioritize your final core values.

Core Values

List four or more values (from the list in Step 1) in order of importance to you:

1. _HEALTH - INDEPEND_
2. _FAMILY/CONTACT ② OTHERS_
3. _WILDERNESS ACTIVITEY_
4. _INTEGRITY RESPECT COMPE TENCE_
5. _ACTIVETY ? TRAVEL_
6. _____
7. _____
8. _____

Step 3: Evaluate how important your financial objectives are in relation to the four values you selected:

 More important than my financial objectives

_____ Equally important as my financial objectives

_____ Less important than my financial objectives

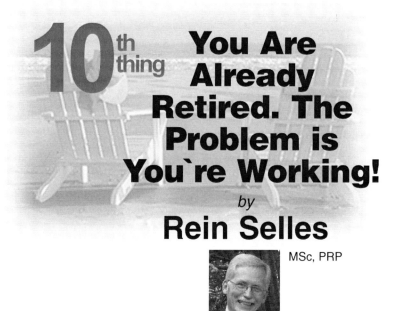

10th thing You Are Already Retired. The Problem is You're Working!

by
Rein Selles
MSc, PRP

"I dreamed a thousand paths...I woke and walked my old one." ~ CHINESE PROVERB

Photograph by Johanna Selles

A path is a strong metaphor for a life plan. The plan or path can be understood to have a beginning and an end. One could enter the path at various points along the way. If the destination is not yet clear, one thing is certain: the path itself sets the direction that the individual is walking.

Your plan to retire may be based on one of two paths. For some retirement is seen as a new beginning, and for others, it is not so much a radical change in lifestyle but rather an extension of the life they are living.

171

RETIREMENT AS A NEW BEGINNING

In the retirement conversations of my clients, there is a very real belief that life can begin anew. For them, retirement represents the possibility of reinventing oneself, of taking a fork in the path that leads to a new direction. This radical shift in lifestyle can come about in a number of ways:

Follow a Dream

Dreams reflect those parts of your personal reality that are yet unfulfilled. Some examples are:

~ To learn to play an instrument

~ To complete your education to a desired level

~ To study and document your roots

~ To see a part of the world that, for you, represents the last frontier

~ To start your own business.

Sharing Your Dreams

A participant at a retirement education class at the University of Alberta proposed an interesting technique to build success. He said, *"The act of talking the plan is the art of bringing it about."* If you are struggling with potential ideas about retirement, ask a friend or family member to be a listening ear.

Sometimes, sharing a plan also invites critique. The goal for the listener is to help the planner move forward. That may also mean that the planner has to learn to let go of a dream when good advice and information indicate that the reality of one's situation cannot support the dream.

> A teacher in Red Deer came to me out of frustration with her partner. Disabled by a medical condition 10 years earlier, her partner had established a pattern of living that was based on his comfort level and her absence. After her retirement she turned to him and said, *"Let's travel."* His response was, *"If you want to go, take off!"* I pointed out that it was not her frustration with her partner that was the issue, but the potential loss of her dream to travel together. Eventually, she followed her dream but with a friend instead of her partner.

There are two cautions I would give those who wish to follow their dreams:

a. Rather than waiting until you retire, see if you can bring your dream to reality sooner. Health changes, the loss of a partner or family member or the ever-changing value of market-based assets could destroy the opportunity to fulfill a dream.

b. Age differences between spouses can create an artificial time zone. Those who retire first can be heard to say, *"I need to wait until my partner retires."* - an idea that's often supported by those who keep working, *"Oh, we'll do that when I retire!"* Don't waste your opportunities – learn to retire in the present, even if one of you is still working!

If you want to talk through your ideas with a professional, seek out the services of a professional life coach. These individuals are trained to help you build a plan based on your dreams and point to areas where you can find further resources.

Relocate

Sunshine and warm weather are significant lures to residents in northern climates. When the temperature drops below freezing and the leaves are off the trees, many northerners may find it hard to find a positive reason to stay in place at retirement.

From a planning perspective, there may be a very narrow window in which plans for moving and staying become critical. Once you retire, any interest in moving outside the community may diminish, reflecting a strong desire for stability rather than for change. For pre-retirees, decisions to relocate seem to coincide with the retirement experience and that could present problems.

Rob and Jane

Rob had a dream – to build a lakefront cottage at a popular resort where he and his family had spent their holidays for the past 20 years. His partner, Jane, however, was quite content in their renovated bungalow in the city. Their home had been carefully redecorated over many years and Jane had developed close ties with neighbours and friends. At his retirement, Rob convinced Jane to sell the house and move to the lake resort. Midway during the construction of his dream home, Rob developed a severe medical problem. At the same time, Jane, unable to manage the loss of her friends, became very depressed. Selling their property at a loss, the couple returned to the city. While Jane's first choice was to return to her old home, she and Rob now live a block away and wait for the day that it will come on the market. Rob is back at work.

Our relationship to our home is a very personal one and can have the following characteristics:

- ~ Long residency
- ~ Family associations and memories
- ~ Sweat equity (the time and effort given to making the house a "home")
- ~ Neighbours and neighbourhood support
- ~ Ownership (in the case of home owners).

For those who have struggled for many years with seemingly endless mortgage payments, the satisfaction of finally owning one's home is a significant reason to stay.

On the other hand, retirement may present an opportunity to move:

- ~ To be closer to family and/or friends
- ~ To an area that supports a personal goal (hunting, fishing, sports)
- ~ To a location with a more relaxed pace (rural or cottage living)
- ~ Away from cold temperatures and snow.

Preparing Yourself To Move

Do a trial run - While you are researching your ideal location, be sure to rehearse living in that community. By using vacation time or a leave of absence to rent or "house-sit", you gain personal knowledge of the community, real estate opportunities, the resources available and the sense of community among residents.

Pre-position yourself – Inflation is a difficult issue in areas that are popular for retirement. I have suggested that, once a community is selected, pre-retirees purchase property and rent it out. Once the owners are ready to retire and make their move, the value of the rental will normally have kept pace with inflation in the community allowing for either:

- ~ A sale with the resulting capital used to purchase a newer home; or

- ~ A move into the rental making it your principal residence.

If you decide this is a good strategy for your own retirement plan, talk to a professional financial planner or accountant about the implications for capital gains tax when you sell a secondary property or change the use of an income or recreational property.

Become part of the community – Some moves fail because new residents can't break into the community. What seems like an open and hospitable community during a visit can close down once the tourists leave. To combat a potential sense of isolation, take a day in a week and become a volunteer. I suggest three potential volunteer activities that could give you an "in":

- ~ Volunteer at the local hospital or health care facility – You are going to be meeting other volunteers who are retired and who have a very good working knowledge of community resources – especially when you are going to be looking for a new doctor!

Volunteer as a *"meals-on-wheels"* driver – In addition to getting to know your community, you will be meeting long-term residents who have excellent knowledge of the community, its history and its problems. The trick is to get out of their home and back to your route before the rest of the food is cold!

- ~ Serve on a municipal committee or board – Most municipalities will post notices asking residents to volunteer for a term. This is a great way to get to know the issues of your new community and meet those who are committed to improving the lifestyle of residents.

Watch the tax rates – Canada uses one day of residence (December 31) in any province or territory to establish your combined federal and provincial or territorial tax rate for that year. That means you need to determine the difference in tax rates between locations before making your plans to move:

- ~ If the tax rate in your retirement location is higher than in your current location, you would wait until January 1 of the year following your retirement to move.

~ If the tax rate in your retirement location is lower than in your current location, you would move before December 31 in the year you retire.

Relocating internationally – There are some Canadian retirees who have elected to move beyond Canada's borders to other parts of the world. There are common themes that form the basis for such moves:

~ Relocating to a holiday location permanently (for the climate or environment)

~ Moving to a country where foreign income is not taxed (leaving more currency in your pocket)

~ Taking up residence in a country where the cost of living is much lower (allowing for a higher standard of living in retirement)

~ Moving closer to family.

The challenge lies in the preparation and experience. I have heard of very good experiences and ones that would make your hair turn greyer. Do your homework! There will be implications for:

~ **Health Care** – There could potentially be problems with access to services as you age.

~ **Taxes** – Income generated within Canada is subject to tax (according to international treaties) for non-residents. Remember, if you leave Canada it doesn't mean that the Canada Revenue Agency loses interest in your affairs. I would recommend that you talk to qualified professionals who specialize in international tax for the country you are moving to. Also, check the Canada Revenue Agency's website for information on leaving Canada at **www.cra.gc.ca.**

~ **Estate planning** – Your affairs at death will be governed under the laws of the jurisdiction where the majority of your activities of life take place. Consult with a qualified professional in that jurisdiction and review all legal and estate provisions to ensure that your wishes can be fulfilled.

~ **Asset management** – The Canada Revenue Agency will take the approach that all capital assets are sold at fair market value once you leave (or sever all ties with) Canada. That could mean that some assets are subject to capital gains tax. Active management of investments by advisors for clients who are non-resident could be problematic depending on the rules. Both your chartered accountant and financial planner should be able to guide you.

Explore The World

There is a small group of retirees in Canada who dream of exploring the world by road, sea or air.

Mary

Mary's dream for retirement was to work on a cruise ship and travel the world. With a background in retail management and an interest in fine jewelry, she forwarded her resume to a variety of cruise lines. When the offer of employment came, Mary had to make a number of decisions:

~ *The sale of her personal residence.*

~ *The storage of her personal property on the assumption that she would return to that community in the future.*

~ *Appointment of a trusted advisor to manage her financial affairs in her absence.*

~ *Arrangements with family and friends.*

Mary's plan was to spend 10 years of her retirement in this lifestyle before returning to her community.

Preparing Yourself

This type of retirement plan relies on three factors to be successful:

a. Your health continues to allow you to remain active. The greatest likelihood for this is while you are in the first stage of retirement (55 to 70 years old).

~ Have a method for ensuring that medical professionals have access to your records in the event of an emergency.

~ If you have a travel partner, take your personal directive with you. While such documents are generally specific to the jurisdiction in which they are created, the fact that you took this step may help your partner successfully become your care advocate, if the need arises.

~ Contact your health care provider to determine the implications of travel outside of Canada both in terms of the need for additional coverage and restrictions under the Canada Health Act for absences longer than six months.

b. You have a community to return to once the mobile lifestyle ends (and it will). If you are planning to use your existing community and home as the base for your mobile travels, retain your principal residence and related benefits of living in that province or territory.

If you need the proceeds of the sale of your property to finance your mobile retirement, you will still need to be *"resident"* – particularly for health care, estate and tax purposes. Check with a lawyer to determine how best to ensure that your principal residence (or primary domicile) is in the location where you wish to reside.

You may also need to check on residency rules in the location you are visiting. The United States, for example, carefully monitors the number of days present to determine if non-residents should be required to file a statement of worldwide income with the Internal Revenue Service.

c. The supporting networks of family and/or friends are still in place when you return. I think the most difficult aspect in mobile retirements is the nature of change. Friends, family and communities continue to change in our absence. At the same time, our memory and expectations of people may remain frozen in time. Coming back, after a long absence, you may find:

~ Friends have moved on to create new relationships with others;

~ The common interests you shared with others are no longer holding you together;

~ Family relationships have grown, and old methods of contact and communication are no longer appropriate or wanted;

~ You seem more a stranger than when you were a visitor on your travels.

~ If you sold your home, the cost of living has appreciated the value of housing to the point where buying a new home is no longer practical.

Perhaps the answer will lie in re-engaging yourself. You will also not be the same person who left years ago. Look to see where you can offer yourself in service and friendship, and new relationships and feelings of *"home"* will likely return.

RETIREMENT AS AN EXTENSION OF A LIFE WELL-LIVED

While some Canadians will find success in planning retirement as a new beginning, many more Canadians will try to continue the lifestyles to which they have become accustomed. When participants ask me, *"Can I maintain my lifestyle when I retire?"*, I am just as likely to return with a counter question, *"How would you know you had a lifestyle worth maintaining?"*

The challenge in planning your retirement is to <u>maximize your choices</u> – to get the most out of life. That process begins with an evaluation of your present lifestyle. Unfortunately, we have very few tools in the retirement planning field that can indicate, at a personal level, whether a person's lifestyle is functioning at optimum levels.

To solve this problem, **Dr. James Lynch** of Eugene, Oregon, a pioneer in the field of retirement education, proposed a method for evaluation of lifestyle that used 10 components. I would also like to acknowledge my colleague, **Mary Holder**, RN, MSc, PRP, who contributed to the development of this exercise for Canadians. This exercise is shown on the following page.

Measuring The Quality Of Your Life
In The Present - Exercise

In the exercise below, you are presented with 10 areas of lifestyle in which you are currently making decisions. The question is, *"Am I happy with the lifestyle I have chosen at this point in my life?"* Evaluate each area and give it a rating based on your personal satisfaction from a scale of one (no satisfaction) to five (high satisfaction). Totaling your score is not necessary.

_____ **Leisure** – the time you make available for leisure pursuits, and the interests and activities you have chosen to pursue when leisure opportunities arise.

_____ **Housing** – the type of housing you live in, its location in the community, your neighbours and the degree of maintenance and upkeep required.

_____ **Self-Worth** – your sense of confidence, self-esteem and feelings of self-worth.

_____ **Health** – your current health status, your personal commitment to maintaining and improving your health, and your access to health care information and resources.

_____ **Finances** – the sufficiency of your income to meet your cash flow requirements, your ability to save, your effective use of debt and credit when needed, your understanding of the financial system, and your ability to access professional help if needed.

_____ **Quality of Significant Relationships** - your perception of your relationships with those close to you including a partner, family members, friends or other acquaintances and the adequacy of your support network.

_____ **Work and Career** – your satisfaction with your work and the adjustments you have made with career choices in your adult life.

_____ **Balance** – the degree to which your goals are being achieved at personal, family and work levels.

_____ **Adjusting to Change** – your sense of how well you are managing with changes, events or transitions in your life so far.

_____ **Legal and Estate** – the availability of up-to-date legal documents that allow those you have selected as administrators to effectively manage your finances and lifestyle decisions in the event of your diminished capacity or death.

Date This Exercise Was Completed _____

Did you write the date you completed the exercise? This last step is important if you wish to have a comparison to your lifestyle when retired. There is a second copy of this lifestyle evaluation at the end of the chapter. Once you have retired, try the exercise again and see whether your lifestyle in retirement has improved. If you are experiencing problems, the comparison will immediately point to where the problem in your lifestyle is.

The Relationship of Your Present Lifestyle to Retirement
There is a Chinese proverb that indicates the relationship of your present lifestyle to the one that you will experience in retirement:

> *"If you don't change direction, you could end up where you are heading!"*

Areas of your life with low satisfaction today are not likely to improve with retirement. You aren't happy with your home? Wait until you are in it another 10 hours a day! Retirement, in a very real way, has the effect of enhancing life when it is good and making things worse when it isn't.

Planning Outcomes – The idea of *"maintaining your lifestyle"* carries the intent that what works today will also work for you in the future. It is more likely, however, that events in life may require changes in lifestyle. I ask participants in my workshops to try the following as an example of planning outcomes:

Step 1: Take your age today, and add 30 years to your age. _____

Step 2: Take the age of your current home and add 30 years _____

Outcome – Are you in the right housing at that age?

Yes _____ **No** _____

If you said, *"No"*, it shows how the environment and your needs may change over time. The question in planning becomes, *"When will I move?"* and *"What kind of housing would create the best environment for me in the future?"*. The research for that move can be done at any time. Sometimes, when people pursue this form of planning in earnest, moves may occur well before the need – an ideal outcome.

What follows is a review of the 10 lifestyle components used in the exercise but with a view of outcomes in retirement.

Leisure – Including Meaningful Interests and Activities and Effective Time Management

For most of us, life is busy and we are engaged in a variety of interests and activities. In order to contribute to our life satisfaction, these interests and activities need to meet certain criteria. They must be meaningful, purposeful and rewarding.

Time management is a concern for most individuals. There never seems to be enough time to accomplish all the tasks we set for ourselves. It is often assumed that one doesn't have to think about time management in retirement because there will be so much free time available. Time management is just as important in retirement but the issue is not quantity, it is quality. How well will you make the best use of the time available?

Living Arrangements

"Home" satisfaction is an important life choice and consideration in overall life satisfaction. Where you live is not always a personal choice as it can be dictated by career, employment, finances, access to schools, etc. What is important is that your needs are met. For some, it may mean being close to family, for others access to certain community facilities. It is often assumed that retirement represents a time of considerable change and that moving is part of that change. To move or not at or in retirement is a choice which will require careful examination.

Feelings of Self Worth, Esteem and Confidence

Everyone has a sense of self-image. Feelings of self-worth, esteem and confidence are influenced by what we do, who we do it with, how well we think we do, how well others think we do, and how others respond and relate to us. Roles that we take on in life contribute a great deal to our sense of self. For example, retirees have a major role adjustment from that of the worker to that of the retiree. For those unprepared for retirement, there can be a lowered self-image while one adjusts to the role of retiree.

Current Health Status

Good health allows the opportunity for greater participation whereas poor health creates restrictions to lifestyle choice. Health, a holistic commodity, is a non-renewable resource. An individual must take responsibility for effective health management strategies throughout a lifetime. Retirees suggest that good health is one of the most important factors contributing to satisfaction in retirement.

Financial Security and Your Ability to Manage Resources Effectively
Money is a basic commodity which has considerable influence on the quality of lifestyle achieved. Financial resources are subject to the impact of external, uncontrolled factors such as inflation or market changes. Consequently, financial planning and management are necessary to ensure maintenance of your desired lifestyle. This is particularly important in preparing for retirement because of a more fixed and reduced income.

Quality of Significant Relationships (Spouse, Family, Friends, Other) and Adequacy of Social Support System
Generally, we want and need people in our lives. We seek quality relationships and need to know that there are supports for us when need arises. Quality relationships require commitment, cooperation and effective communication. Retirees cite involvement with people as the most important factor in retirement satisfaction.

Work/Career Satisfaction and Adjustments
Not everyone is gainfully employed, but everyone has a career. A career is what one is doing at a given point in time such as paid employment, management of the home, community involvement or world traveler! What is important for life satisfaction is that one feels challenged and can adapt to any adjustments required. There are multiple options for a "career" in retirement, but one must plan ahead.

Balancing Career/Personal Goals
The greatest life satisfaction is achieved when there is an equitable balance between the *"shoulds"* (demands and responsibilities) and what the individual does for one's own personal growth and development. Too often, there is a tendency to short-change oneself and allow too much *"push/pull"* which contributes to increased stress and dissatisfaction.

Adjustment to Change
Life is a series of changes, events and transitions, some of which are predictable and others which are not. Individuals must be flexible and adaptable to cope with change and require effective coping strategies to deal with the stress involved. Ability to control stress and not have stress control you is the key to successful management of change.

Legal and Estate Plans
This is a very important component of financial planning and management which refers specifically to significant loss - the issue of death and bereavement. Death is inevitable in life and requires both

financial and emotional preparation. Planning in the area of finances, wills, and funeral arrangements, can have very positive and beneficial effects for the survivor.

Summary
Making appropriate individual choices in each of these 10 areas is essential if you wish to achieve happiness and overall life satisfaction. Regular on-going assessment of these areas will ensure that your quality lifestyle is maintained.

DETERMINING SUCCESS IN RETIREMENT PLANS
The challenge in all forms of planning is to make decisions in such a way that the likelihood of success improves. In an ideal world, we would all get a chance to practice retirement first and then, based on what we've learned, make our plans. The premise set out in this chapter is that life is our rehearsal, and the skills and knowledge we develop over our lifetime are also the tools of an effective retirement plan.

Let me indicate how your present lifestyle choices can influence your retirement lifestyle:

The Home You Are in Is Most Likely Going to Be Your Retirement Residence
When I ask participants in my workshops, *"How many of you plan to remain in your current home at retirement?"* approximately two-thirds will indicate their preference for staying in place. Your chances of success will increase if you take into account the following issues:

Plan home maintenance and upkeep
Most homes have a 15-year maintenance cycle. That means, if you renovated at retirement, you may be revisiting some of these expenditures when you are in your mid-70s or early 80s. It is at that point that all inflation will catch up with you. Labour and materials will have increased over time while assets may have depreciated (particularly if investment income was drawn off or growth was below the rate of inflation). Your willingness <u>at that point</u> to invest more capital into maintaining your home will be a pivotal issue in the decision to stay or move.

Know what you can't take with you
If you ever wondered how much of your material possessions you would have to eliminate in that next move, count on 70 to 80%. There are two suggestions I would offer:

1. Begin a process of downsizing your possessions well before you retire. A box a week over 52 weeks can significantly lower your stress levels and eliminate the need to pay for transport and/or storage.

2. If you plan to move and you have the resources available, take only those items that have meaning for you, and sell or give away everything else. Come into the new space without the burden of trying to fit old furniture in spaces for which the items were never designed.

Eliminate barriers to independent living inside and outside your home

Physical limitations with age may make staying in place more difficult. Look for potential obstacles to independent living and eliminate them ahead of retirement. Canada Mortgage and Housing Corporation has some excellent printed resources to help Canadians examine this issue.

Retirement Can Offer an Opportunity to Renew Your Commitment To a More Healthy Lifestyle

When behaviour that contributes to wellbeing is difficult to initiate or maintain during your career, retirement can present an ideal opportunity to *"change your lifestyle"* in a positive way. The break in routine and structure opens a path in which other choices become possible.

1. As Jim notes, perhaps the best way to begin is with a full physical. Know the problem(s) you are going to try to resolve. Your physician may also be in the best position to know how such changes should be initiated and the kind of resources that may be necessary.

2. Set out a schedule that is easy to maintain. For example, it may be easier to begin an exercise program when it is the first activity of the day.

3. Use the services of a coach to help you *"stage"* your plans so that goals are more easily attained and progress can be measured.

4. While such changes can be accomplished on one's own, there is also value in joining a group that shares the same goal. Such groups have the added advantage of trained leaders who can help overcome problems.

Recognize the Potential Changes in Social Contact That Will Come at Retirement
There is a very good exercise that will help you recognize how much change you may experience. Pick a day of your work week and from the time you get up, measure the amount of contact you have with colleagues, co-workers and members of the general public. Next, on a day off or a weekend, measure again the contact you have with people – including those who are close to you. While contact with those outside of your immediate family and friends will decrease, contact with those close to you will increase. Ask yourself:

~ Are the relationships you have with those close to you sufficient to meet your needs as you retire?

~ What activities or choices can you make in retirement that will increase your contact with those who share common interests or allow you to feel part of a community?

~ Changes in health may limit our ability to participate actively in our community. That knowledge may also require a more careful consideration of housing options at retirement. Do you need a community, such as an adult housing complex, to help build lost relationships from work?

The Retirement Party Can Be Both a Beginning, and an Ending
Sometimes it is hard to figure out whose needs are being served in such events. I have always felt that the retirement party is similar, in many ways, to a wake:

~ Those who know you the least seem to have the most to say about you;

~ There seems to be a lot of looking at watches as if the event is to be endured rather than enjoyed;

~ People seem to focus around the food table;

~ A *"slab"* cake is served with your name and the word *"Farewell"* or *"Goodbye"* on it;

~ Gifts are more likely to represent the interest of the buyer than the receiver;

~ The last person in the room is the one who should have been the first to leave!

I think there is room in a retirement plan for a graceful exit and a joyful entrance. Give thought to both:

The *"work is finished"* party is an event organized on your behalf by others. Plan a way to recognize those who have meant the most to you. A letter, card or small gift that indicates what value you placed on the relationship is a good way to leave those you care about. Some pre-retirees will dread the idea of giving a *"speech"* at such events. Make it fun for yourself. If you don't like speaking in public, use a video with prepared notes and show the video instead. And yes, you may be the last person standing in the room when it is over.

The *"retirement is beginning"* party is an event you organize for those who will share this new lifestyle with you and could include some of your colleagues from work with whom you hope to maintain contact in retirement. For fun, ask those who come to bring along one small item that they think is essential to your success.

Test Your Retirement Plans
Learn to test your retirement plans for three specific components:

1. *"Will my life have **purpose?**"* As you evaluate your future lifestyle, are there choices that you can be passionate about? In the absence of purpose, life loses its drive and forward momentum. There has to be more to get you up in the morning than pressure on your bladder!

2. *"Will what I choose to do in retirement be **meaningful** to me?"* In the absence of meaning there is a real risk – that what you do becomes boring.

3. *"Will I have a **structure** in my retirement that allows me to manage the increase in time?"* While many pre-retirees will point to the fact that retirement represents an opportunity to be free of the constraints of time, there is still a need to maintain a pattern that allows you to order basic elements of life (meals, contact with others, recreation, etc.).

Tailored for Success
A few years ago the Human Resources Department in one of Alberta's cities gave me the opportunity to teach a refresher class to a group that had previously taken a pre-retirement planning workshop. One of the participants came over to me to explain that her husband had, since the last workshop, retired.

"How is he doing?" I asked.

"He is so successful!" she said.

"That is an interesting choice of words - what do you mean by successful?"

"*He wears his retirement like a coat,*" she said. *"It fits him perfectly."*

When her husband appeared, I indicated that his wife felt he had demonstrated success in retirement. I asked him what he attributed that success to.

He said, *"I do a little of everything!"*

A perfect fit. Pieces of activity learned over a lifetime sewn together in such a way that it takes the shape of who you are – retired!

Retirement is a Life Within a Life

Jim Yih

When I think of retirement as a path, I think of another common saying: *"Any path will get you somewhere."* But is that *"somewhere"* where you want to go?

In my experience, I often see people's retirement planning fitting into the thought process: *"Life is busy."* I think to a certain extent, we are all busy people. We all have busy lives and we all have lots to do. As a result, we are all, to some extent, creatures of habit. Now I'm not saying that you may not be adventurous from time to time and you won't try new things or be impulsive; but, routines and patterns of life are comfortable. For example, how many of you drive to work the same way every single day? How many of you have 250 TV channels and you watch the same 10 most of the time? How many of you have a wardrobe of clothes but you wear the same 20% most of the time? How many of you go to the same restaurants and order the same items off the menu most of the time? If you think about it, isn't it really disappointing to go out for dinner to try a new restaurant, pay a lot of money for a lousy meal, lousy service or a lousy experience? And if this happens we often go back to our favourites, because then we know what to expect.

WHAT MAKES RETIREMENT TRULY SUCCESSFUL?

Habits are a significant part of our lives. How many of us are on a path heading somewhere but not really knowing if the path is heading to a place where we really want to go? It may be comfortable, convenient, easy or just the way it is because of the routines and habits in our lives. In other words, how many of us are living a life but living it in the present and not taking the time to plan the future life that we would like to live?

Planning to me is simply looking down that path to see what the future holds. It's about creating some predictability about the future. It's about thinking forward and having something to **retire to** as opposed to a retirement based on what you are **retiring from**.

So remember, retirement can be anything you want it to be. You simply need to figure out what you want it to be. The answers lie within you. When you have developed a retirement card (Exercise 1) that makes you smile and makes you really excited because it represents who you want to be when you grow up, then you are well on your way to a successful retirement because true success comes in planning your lifestyle.

Retirement planning is also about numbers and as a result, you will need to have some future projections about your income, expenses, assets and liabilities. You can't plan for the future without some projections. As you have learned throughout this book, one of the most difficult parts of retirement planning is the assumptions you will need to make about the future, but don't let that be a hurdle to your planning. Too often, planning loses its personal focus because we use too many rules of thumb or have a difficult time with the assumptions like life expectancy, inflation and rates of return. The best plans are ones that are well thought out and are personal in nature.

Everyone I meet at my retirement planning courses says, *"I wish I would have started my planning sooner,"* which means that planning should never be delayed. It's never too late to start, and some planning is better than no planning at all. You can live your life by chance or by choice; the difference is how much you plan.

Remember that the best time to retire is when you are ready. And despite the messages that being ready is all about the money, true success comes in recognizing that it's not all about the money. True success comes in understanding your lifestyle needs, and the sweet spot of retirement planning is when your lifestyle matches your money. In other words successful retirement planning happens in the harmonization of two key issues – money issues and lifestyle issues.

RETIREMENT IS A LIFE WITHIN A LIFE

When I read Chapter 10, it reminded me that retirement is a life within a life. Although retirement can often be the *"dream,"* I think retirement is more the extension of the life you are already living. All of the issues that you will face in retirement, you face now including leisure activities, living arrangements, social structure and relationships, your health, work activities, finances and money. Feeling good about life and finding the balance are what we all seek.

The best way to live a successful life in the future is to live your life now as if you were retired and living the best years of your life right here and now.

In the end, it's your choice. You can keep living the life that you are living and stay on the path you are on, but remember, any path will get you somewhere. The question remains, *"Is that the somewhere you want to go to?"* As Patricia says, taking action is by far the toughest step because it initiates commitment. But it also initiates change. It may help to remember that the definition of insanity is doing the same things over and over and over again and expecting different results.

I leave you with one final story – one of my favourite stories about retirement. I think it captures the essence of my retirement beliefs:

The Management Consultant and the Fisherman

One day a consultant was on a fishing holiday in the Caribbean. As he was sitting on the docks, a local fisherman came in with his catch of the morning. The consultant noticed the catch and asked the fisherman, *"How long did it take you to catch those fish?"*

The fisherman replied, *"Not very long."*

"Why didn't you stay out longer to catch more fish then?" asked the consultant.

"Because I have more than enough to satisfy the needs of my family and I," said the fisherman.

"What will you do with the rest of your day?" asked the consultant.

"Every day is the same. I sleep late, fish a little in the mornings, go home and eat with my family, play with the kids and take an afternoon nap underneath a coconut tree. After supper I go to the community hall to be with my friends. We laugh, play games, dance to music, and sing songs. I have a happy life," said the fisherman.

The consultant said, *"I have an MBA from Harvard and I can help you have a better life. You should go fish longer so you can catch more fish. You can sell the extra fish and with the money you can buy a bigger boat. That boat will bring you more money so you can buy a second boat and a third until you have a fleet of boats. Instead of selling the fish to a middle man, you can sell the fish directly to the processing plants or maybe even open a plant of your own. You can leave this little island and move to the big city where you will find more contacts for your successful business."*

"How long will this take?" asked the fisherman.

"Maybe 10 or 20 years," said the consultant.

"And after that?" asked the fisherman.

"This is where it gets really interesting," said the consultant. *"You can then sell the shares of your company for millions and millions of dollars."*

"And after that?"

"You can leave the city and move to an island where you can fish everyday, spend time with family and friends, and sleep occasionally under a coconut tree."

Hey, Can I Have a Do-Over?

Patricia French

Have you heard of a *"do-over?"* This rite of childhood came into play as you learned a new skill like hitting a ball. A do-over was an amazing capacity we had as kids to defy the space-time continuum and roll back the game clock and try again. If you struck out, a kind and supportive adult or older sibling would give you a do-over. The error did not count against you in the game, and you could hold your head high, get back into a batter's stance, and swing for the fences once again.

Why then can we not give ourselves the same benefit when considering our retirement plans? So often adults tend to see mistakes as failures, yet the message we got as children, and gave to our children, was practice, practice, practice. Finding *"your retirement"* may take practice, practice, practice.

The media has inundated us with compelling imagery of a retirement lifestyle of activity, affluence and personal fulfilment. There is <u>never</u> an air of *"Oops, what have I done?"* or *"Phooey, I'm bored!,"* or *"Eek, the market downturn really hurt!"* The perception is that retirement is an event, like turning a page in a book and beginning a new chapter. This conveys an added pressure that when making your decision to retire there is no room for error. For many people retirement is a process or evolution. So much will change, that to expect to make perfect decisions at one point in time that will remain true over the decades of retirement, is not only unrealistic, it can feel overwhelming. A new chapter? What if you would rather start a new book?

The decision to leave paid employment and draw pension or other retirement income is a practical way to define retirement. A great deal of thought goes into making the decision and the assumption is we are adequately informed and financially and emotionally ready to embark on the next phase of our lives. However, we will not always get it right the first time.

Prepare to give yourself permission for a do-over. There are two main reasons you may want a do-over. First, you may have taken the wrong path, feel regret about a decision, or sense something is missing or lost. Second, you may have experienced something that connected with you so deeply that you simply want to relive it. No doubt you may find that something about your retirement lifestyle is in conflict with your values, strengths, or interests.

Sports analysts make a good living out of reviewing the action on the field or ice. When you want a do-over, you need to step back and review the plays you have made and take inventory of what worked and what didn't.

I THOUGHT I KNEW WHO I WANTED TO BE WHEN I RETIRED!

Finding Balance

Consider Paul and Evelyn, retirees who dreamed of travelling around North America by RV only to discover that the joy of the open road started to dissolve after only a few months of adventure. RVing had long been how they spent family vacation time and it continued after their kids left home, so they had not built their retirement lifestyle around an untapped ambition. But four weeks of annual vacation on the road is a far cry from six months or year-round. They were surprised to discover how much they missed the family and social connections of home, and that the gap could not be filled with networking websites and e-mail. For Paul and Evelyn, their do-over was to hold on to the facets of the RV lifestyle which fit like a glove, but re-evaluate to find the right balance between home and away.

Don't Tell Anyone, But I Miss Work!

It's okay to admit you miss working, but can you express why? Many of us get more than a pay cheque from our work. You likely don't miss early starts or parking battles, but you may miss other aspects.

Do you miss your job or working?

Do you miss working or the activity?

Do you miss working or the regular routine?

Do you miss working or the additional income?

Do you miss working or your colleagues?

Do you miss your colleagues or a social outlet?

If you can isolate or identify the reasons why, you can redefine your retirement lifestyle to fit you better and give you greater satisfaction.

Getting Recharged

Heather retired at age 60. She had done the math and was confident her retirement income would provide her with the lifestyle she desired. For the last five years of her career she found herself counting down the remaining days until her retirement date, going so far as to download a ticker for her laptop that tracked the days, hours, minutes and seconds left till *"the big day."* Once retired, she found herself lacking vision or focus. Something was missing and it took some introspection to pinpoint the void. She realized the last few years of her career were about putting in time and her contentment at work had faded. Much to her surprise she missed work, not what work had become, but a time when she was doing project management. She had experienced such success and sense of purpose, that finding part-time contract work in project management filled the void in retirement. Her do-over was rolling back the clock to relive a time when work charged her sense of spirit.

Feeling Productive

Charlie experienced *"serial retirement."* He retired … several times, but consistently found himself back working. He returned to both paid and volunteer work. Money was not the issue, but a profound connection to productive work he held from his early teens. Over time he reassessed the value gained from working and both the hours and nature of work changed as other retirement roles became a greater priority. His retirement lifestyle may never have made the cover of a retirement industry brochure, but it was just as valid a choice. His do-over met his wish to feel needed and productive in retirement.

Retrieving Relationships

It may not be the work you miss, it could be the people. Then the question becomes, is it your old colleagues or social contact in general? Even if you were close to your colleagues, those relationships change when you retire, particularly if you were the only one to retire. With endless ways to give the social aspect of your retirement lifestyle a shot in the arm, returning to work need not be the answer. The do-over is not retrieving relationships that were limited to the workplace, but creating new ones based on you…retired.

I THOUGHT I COULD AFFORD IT, BUT THINGS CHANGED.

Despite best-laid plans, it is possible to misjudge the resources required to live the lifestyle we sought in retirement and leave work prematurely. Changes in the market, economy, or our needs can also cause our flow of resources to come up short. Income from work can augment lifestyle as long as health permits, but solutions which achieve balance by reducing expenditures are often more sustainable.

Stepping Up

Debbie was as contented a retiree as you might find. She felt as if she were in the prime of her life. She was financially comfortable, busy, and delighted in the relationship with her precocious seven-year-old granddaughter. Debbie's situation changed when her daughter's marriage ended and her daughter and granddaughter needed both her practical and financial support to rebuild their lives. Debbie wanted to support her daughter's plan to upgrade her education and improve her earning potential, knowing this meant she would take on additional financial demands for a couple of years. She borrowed money to construct a basement suite and returned to work part-time to supplement her income and pay for the renovation. Debbie saw this do-over as an investment in the wellbeing of her family. The revenue suite, that today gave her family a fresh start, would foreseeably provide a revenue stream to step up her retirement earnings for years to come.

Retirement decisions can be sorted between those which can be changed and those which cannot be changed. Thankfully, there are few decisions that are impossible to do-over. Regardless of age, you cannot do-over your decision to draw pension income. Whether it is your employment pension, annuity income, or CPP benefits, once the tap is turned on, it cannot be turned off, even if you do not need the money. At 71 years of age, all streams of pension income must start, so even RRIF income will pour in. You can have a do-over with your RRIF income before age 71, as you can convert it back to an RRSP and again make contributions. An investment professional or financial planner can help resolve the matter of surplus income, but kept in perspective, too much money is not such a bad problem to have. One other area of financial planning does not allow a do-over – insurance. Once you have cancelled that policy, the protection it provided has ended.

In retirement, endorse the childhood rite of the do-over. As a Turkish proverb says, *"No matter how far you have gone on the wrong road, turn back."* Then, review, rework, and redo as needed and feel confident that you can continue to practice, practice, practice to swing for the fences once again!

Exercise Twelve

Making It Personal

Measuring the Quality of Your Life in Retirement

I n the exercise below, you are presented with 10 areas of lifestyle in which you are currently making decisions. The question is, *"Am I happy with the lifestyle I have chosen at this point in my life?"* Evaluate each area and give it a rating based on your personal satisfaction from a scale of one (no satisfaction) to five (high satisfaction). Totaling your score is not necessary.

_____4_____ **Leisure** – the time you make available for leisure pursuits, and the interests and activities you have chosen to pursue when leisure opportunities arise.

_____4_____ **Housing** – the type of housing you live in, its location in the community, your neighbours and the degree of maintenance and upkeep required.

_____4_____ **Self-Worth** – your sense of confidence, self-esteem and feelings of self-worth.

_____3_____ NEED WORK **Health** – your current health status, your personal commitment to maintaining and improving your health, and your access to health care information and resources.

_____4_____ **Finances** – the sufficiency of your income to meet your cash flow requirements, your ability to save, your effective use of debt and credit when needed, your understanding of the financial system, and your ability to access professional help if needed.

_____3_____ NEEDS EFFORT **Quality of Significant Relationships** - your perception of your relationships with those close to you including a partner, family members, friends or other acquaintances and the adequacy of your support network.

_4_   **Work and Career** – your satisfaction with your work and the adjustments you have made with career choices in your adult life.

_4_   **Balance** – the degree to which your goals are being achieved at personal, family and work levels.

_3½_   **Adjusting to Change** – your sense of how well you are managing with changes, events or transitions in your life so far.

_____   **Legal and Estate** – the availability of up-to-date legal documents that allow those you have selected as administrators to effectively manage your finances and lifestyle decisions in the event of your diminished capacity or death.

Date This Exercise Was Completed _____MAY 2016_____

Now compare your scores (retired) to the exercise you completed before retirement to see whether your lifestyle in retirement is equal to or better than your lifestyle before retirement. Low scores indicate areas of dissatisfaction where continued planning and professional guidance may be needed.

In the chart below, we illustrate the different tax brackets and marginal tax rates for each province which includes both provincial and federal tax. The Marginal tax and average tax calculations are based on an example of $50,000 and $100,000 of total taxable income for the year.

2010 Marginal Tax vs Average Tax

British Columbia

Income Lower limit	Income upper limit	marginal tax rate	Tax on $50,000	Tax on $100,000
$ -	$ 10,382	0.00%	$ -	$ -
$ 10,383	$ 18,708	15.00%	$ 1,249	$ 1,249
$ 18,709	$ 29,441	20.06%	$ 2,153	$ 2,153
$ 29,442	$ 35,859	23.26%	$ 1,493	$ 1,493
$ 35,860	$ 40,970	20.06%	$ 1,025	$ 1,025
$ 40,971	$ 71,719	22.70%	$ 6,980	$ 6,980
$ 71,720	$ 81,941	29.70%	$ (6,451)	$ 3,036
$ 81,942	$ 82,342	32.50%		$ 130
$ 82,343	$ 99,987	36.50%		$ 6,440
$ 99,988	$ 127,021	38.29%		$ 10,351
$ 127,022		40.70%		$ (10,998)
		43.70%		
Total Ta			$ 6,448	$ 21,858
Average Tax Rate (%)			12.9%	21.9%
Marginal Tax Rate (%)			29.7%	40.7%

Ontario

Income Lower limit	Income upper limit	marginal tax rate	Tax on $50,000	Tax on $100,000
$ -	$ 10,382	0.00%	$ -	$ -
$ 10,383	$ 13,022	15.00%	$ 396	$ 396
$ 13,023	$ 17,101	25.10%	$ 1,024	$ 1,024
$ 17,102	$ 37,106	20.05%	$ 4,011	$ 4,011
$ 37,107	$ 40,970	24.15%	$ 933	$ 933
$ 40,971	$ 65,344	31.15%	$ 2,813	$ 7,592
$ 65,345	$ 74,214	32.98%		$ 2,925
$ 74,215	$ 76,986	35.39%		$ 981
$ 76,987	$ 81,941	39.41%		$ 1,952
$ 81,942	$ 127,021	43.41%		$ 19,569
$ 127,022		46.41%		
Total T			$ 9,176	$ 39,382
Average Tax Rate (%)			18.4%	39.4%
Marginal Tax Rate (%)			31.2%	43.4%

Alberta

Income Lower limit	Income upper limit	marginal tax rate	Tax on $50,000	Tax on $100,000
$ -	$ 10,382	0.00%	$ -	$ -
$ 10,383	$ 16,775	15.00%	$ 959	$ 959
$ 16,776	$ 40,970	25.00%	$ 6,049	$ 6,049
$ 40,971	$ 81,941	32.00%	$ 2,889	$ 13,110
$ 81,942	$ 127,021	36.00%		$ 6,501
$ 127,022		39.00%		
Total Ta			$ 9,897	$ 26,619
Average Tax Rate (%)			19.8%	26.6%
Marginal Tax Rate (%)			32.0%	36.0%

Quebec

Income Lower limit	Income upper limit	marginal tax rate	Tax on $50,000	Tax on $100,000
$ -	$ 10,382	0.00%	$ -	$ -
$ 10,383	$ 13,070	12.52%	$ 336	$ 336
$ 13,071	$ 38,385	28.52%	$ 7,220	$ 7,220
$ 38,386	$ 40,970	32.52%	$ 840	$ 840
$ 40,971	$ 76,770	38.37%	$ 3,464	$ 13,736
$ 76,771	$ 81,941	42.37%		$ 2,191
$ 81,942	$ 127,021	45.71%		$ 8,254
$ 127,022		48.21%		
Total T			$ 11,861	$ 32,577
Average Tax Rate (%)			23.7%	32.6%
Marginal Tax Rate (%)			38.4%	45.7%

Saskatchewan

Income Lower limit	Income upper limit	marginal tax rate	Tax on $50,000	Tax on $100,000
$ -	$ 10,382	0.00%	$ -	$ -
$ 10,383	$ 13,348	15.00%	$ 445	$ 445
$ 13,349	$ 40,354	26.00%	$ 7,021	$ 7,021
$ 40,355	$ 40,970	28.00%	$ 172	$ 172
$ 40,971	$ 81,941	35.00%	$ 3,160	$ 14,340
$ 81,942	$ 115,297	39.00%		$ 7,043
$ 115,298	$ 127,021	41.00%		
$ 127,022		44.00%		
Total Ta			$ 10,354	$ 28,576
Average Tax Rate (%)			20.7%	28.6%
Marginal Tax Rate (%)			35.0%	39.0%

This chart is brought to you by:

WealthWebGurus.com
Your resource center to build, protect and manage wealth.

The content is for general information purposes only and does not constitute advice. The content was provided by MacKenzie Financial as of the date of writing; however, we give no assurance or warranty regarding the accuracy, timeliness, or applicability of any of the contents. For prudent tax and financial advice, you should always seek the advice of an appropriately qualified professional. All content and information might be changed or updated without notice.

Manitoba

Income Lower limit	Income upper limit	marginal tax rate	Tax on $50,000	Tax on $100,000
$ -	$ 8,134	0.00%	$ -	$ -
$ 8,135	$ 10,382	10.80%	$ 243	$ 243
$ 10,383	$ 31,000	25.80%	$ 5,319	$ 5,319
$ 31,001	$ 40,970	27.75%	$ 2,766	$ 2,766
$ 40,971	$ 67,000	34.75%	$ 3,138	$ 9,045
$ 67,001	$ 81,941	39.40%		$ 5,886
$ 81,942	$ 127,021	43.40%		$ 7,837
$ 127,022		43.40%		
		46.40%		
Total Ta			$ 11,466	$ 31,097
Average Tax Rate (%)			22.9%	31.1%
Marginal Tax Rate (%)			39.4%	43.4%

2010 Marginal Tax vs Average Tax

Nova Scotia

Income		Earnings	Tax on	Tax on
Lower limit	upper limit		$50,000	$100,000
$ -	$ 10,382	0.00%	$ -	$ -
$ 10,383	$ 11,644	15.00%	$ 189	$ 189
$ 11,645	$ 15,000	23.79%	$ 798	$ 798
$ 15,001	$ 21,000	28.79%	$ 1,727	$ 1,727
$ 21,001	$ 29,590	23.79%	$ 2,043	$ 2,043
$ 29,591	$ 40,970	29.95%	$ 3,408	$ 3,408
$ 40,971	$ 59,180	36.95%	$ 3,336	$ 6,728
$ 59,181	$ 81,369	38.67%		$ 8,580
$ 81,370	$ 81,941	40.34%		$ 230
$ 81,942	$ 93,000	44.34%		$ 4,903
$ 93,001	$ 127,021	45.25%		$ 3,167
$ 127,022		48.25%		
		Total T	$ 11,502	$ 31,775
	Average Tax Rate (%)		23.0%	31.8%
	Marginal Tax Rate (%)		37.0%	45.3%

Northwest Territories

Income		Earnings	Tax on	Tax on
Lower limit	upper limit		$50,000	$100,000
$ -	$ 10,382	0.00%	$ -	$ -
$ 10,383	$ 12,740	15.00%	$ 354	$ 354
$ 12,741	$ 37,106	20.90%	$ 5,092	$ 5,092
$ 37,107	$ 40,970	23.60%	$ 912	$ 912
$ 40,971	$ 74,214	30.60%	$ 2,763	$ 10,172
$ 74,215	$ 81,941	34.20%		$ 2,642
$ 81,942	$ 120,656	38.20%		$ 6,898
$ 120,657	$ 127,021	40.05%		
$ 127,022		43.05%		
		Total Ta	$ 9,120	$ 26,070
	Average Tax Rate (%)		18.2%	26.1%
	Marginal Tax Rate (%)		30.6%	38.2%

New Brunswick

Income		Earnings	Tax on	Tax on
Lower limit	upper limit		$50,000	$100,000
$ -	$ 10,382	0.00%	$ -	$ -
$ 10,383	$ 14,648	15.00%	$ 640	$ 640
$ 14,649	$ 32,848	30.12%	$ 5,482	$ 5,482
$ 32,849	$ 36,421	25.12%	$ 897	$ 897
$ 36,422	$ 40,970	30.48%	$ 1,386	$ 1,386
$ 40,971	$ 72,843	37.48%	$ 3,384	$ 11,946
$ 72,844	$ 81,941	38.80%		$ 3,530
$ 81,942	$ 118,427	42.80%		$ 7,729
$ 118,428	$ 127,021	43.95%		
$ 127,022		46.95%		
		Total T	$ 11,789	$ 31,609
	Average Tax Rate (%)		23.6%	31.6%
	Marginal Tax Rate (%)		37.5%	42.8%

Yukon

Income		Earnings	Tax on	Tax on
Lower limit	upper limit		$50,000	$100,000
$ -	$ 10,382	0.00%	$ -	$ -
$ 10,383	$ 40,970	22.04%	$ 6,741	$ 6,741
$ 40,971	$ 80,708	31.68%	$ 2,860	$ 12,589
$ 80,709	$ 81,941	32.16%		$ 396
$ 81,942	$ 127,021	38.01%		$ 6,864
$ 127,022		42.40%		
		Total Ta	$ 9,602	$ 26,590
	Average Tax Rate (%)		19.2%	26.6%
	Marginal Tax Rate (%)		31.7%	38.0%

Prince Edward Island

Income		Earnings	Tax on	Tax on
Lower limit	upper limit		$50,000	$100,000
$ -	$ 10,259	0.00%	$ -	$ -
$ 10,260	$ 10,382	9.80%	$ 12	$ 12
$ 10,383	$ 15,000	24.80%	$ 1,145	$ 1,145
$ 15,001	$ 20,000	29.80%	$ 1,490	$ 1,490
$ 20,001	$ 31,984	24.80%	$ 2,972	$ 2,972
$ 31,985	$ 40,970	28.80%	$ 2,588	$ 2,588
$ 40,971	$ 63,969	35.80%	$ 3,232	$ 8,233
$ 63,970	$ 81,941	38.70%		$ 6,955
$ 81,942	$ 98,143	42.70%		$ 6,918
$ 98,144	$ 127,021	44.37%		$ 824
$ 127,022		47.37%		
		Total T	$ 11,439	$ 31,136
	Average Tax Rate (%)		22.9%	31.1%
	Marginal Tax Rate (%)		35.8%	44.4%

Nunavut

Income		Earnings	Tax on	Tax on
Lower limit	upper limit		$50,000	$100,000
$ -	$ 10,382	0.00%	$ -	$ -
$ 10,383	$ 11,714	15.00%	$ 200	$ 200
$ 11,715	$ 40,970	19.00%	$ 5,558	$ 5,558
$ 40,971	$ 81,941	29.00%	$ 2,618	$ 11,881
$ 81,942	$ 127,021	35.00%		$ 6,320
$ 127,022		40.50%		
		Total Ta	$ 8,377	$ 23,960
	Average Tax Rate (%)		16.8%	24.0%
	Marginal Tax Rate (%)		29.0%	35.0%

Newfoundland

Income		Earnings	Tax on	Tax on
Lower limit	upper limit		$50,000	$100,000
$ -	$ 10,382	0.00%	$ -	$ -
$ 10,383	$ 15,132	15.00%	$ 712	$ 712
$ 15,133	$ 16,022	22.70%	$ 202	$ 202
$ 16,023	$ 19,535	38.70%	$ 1,359	$ 1,359
$ 19,536	$ 31,278	22.70%	$ 2,665	$ 2,665
$ 31,279	$ 40,970	27.80%	$ 2,694	$ 2,694
$ 40,971	$ 62,121	34.80%	$ 3,142	$ 7,360
$ 62,122	$ 81,941	37.50%		$ 7,432
$ 81,942	$ 127,021	41.50%		$ 7,494
$ 127,022		44.50%		
		Total T	$ 10,775	$ 29,919
	Average Tax Rate (%)		21.5%	29.9%
	Marginal Tax Rate (%)		27.8%	37.5%

The End?

Congratulations on reaching the end of this book. While some writers pen their acknowledgements at the front of a book, we thought it more appropriate to thank you as a reader for participating in what we hope was a unique learning experience.

We recognize that as you were reading, the experiences and needs of others around you may have come to mind. If you feel that someone might benefit by receiving this book as a gift, make a copy of this page, complete the form below and fax it to the number shown. We will send the book along with a gift card in your name.

Give The Gift of A Retirement Plan -
Fax Completed Form to (866) 571-5532

Please send _____ copy of this book to (Please Print):

Name _____

Address: _____

_____

City/Prov. _____

Postal Code _____

Name to be recorded in the gift card

_____

Date you would like the book to arrive

_____

Please indicate your e-mail or phone for authorization of charges.

_____

Payment will be by **Visa** or **Master Card** once total cost is assessed.

Typical Cost:		
	Book Price	$28.00
	Less Reader Discount	($8.00)
	Sub-Total	$20.00
	GST, Shipping & Handling	$10.00 (Est.)
	Total	$30.00

Retirement / Life Challenge

**All across Canada there are Canadians
wondering if they can retire.**

There are also over 50,000 Canadians
who have stopped wondering
and started planning.

Charting
your Course

Planning for
Personal Freedom

Life and Retirement Planning programs can make a difference at any age. Our goal is to provide a learning environment where you can explore your options with highly trained and experienced resource personnel.

For information on delivery of courses, workshops or conference presentations, contact:

Retirement/Life Challenge Ltd.
9 Elliot Place
St. Albert, Alberta
T8N 5S5
(780) 458-4696

www.retirementchallenge.com

Co-Author: **10 Things** I wish someone had told me about Retirement

Retirement / Life Challenge

Make Retirement the Best Years of Your Life

Rein Selles MSc, PRP

About Us
Corporate Introduction

Courses
(over 45 and under 45)
- 3hrs to 3 days
Keynote presentations
(1-3 hours)

Our Team
Rein Selles
Jim Yih
Patricia French

Download

Book/Products

Resourses

Rein Selles is a Professional Retirement Planner specializing in the area of Lifestyle and Income Planning. Over the past thirty-five years, his experience has covered the full range of retirement lifestyles from those who are well and living in the community to those who are in care. As a teacher, Rein has taught in the faculty of Human Ecology (University of Alberta, Edmonton). In his capacity as a Pre-retirement Educator, he has had the privilege of helping over fifty-six thousand Canadians across Canada plan their retirements through his company, Retirement/Life Challenge Ltd. He was awarded Honorary Life Membership in the Retirement Planners Association of Canada and recognized as a Distinguished Alumni of the University of Waterloo for his contributions to the field.

About Us | Courses | Our Team | Download | Book/Products | Resourses

Co-Author: **10 Things** I wish someone had told me about Retirement

Jim Yih
LIVE WELL • RETIRE HAPPY
CSA, RDB, PRP

Ideas for Success, Wealth & Happiness

Don't miss this!!

About Us
Corporate Introduction

Courses
(over 45 and under 45)
- 3hrs to 3 days
Keynote presentations
(1-3 hours)

Our Team
Rein Selles
Jim Yih
Patricia French

Download

Book/Products

Resourses

Jim Yih is one of Canada's leading experts on wealth and money. Since 1990, Jim has dedicated his career to educating people in the area of retirement planning, personal finance, investing and wealth management through his syndicated column, retirement workshops, fee only consulting and best selling books. Currently, Jim specializes in delivering retirement workshops to help people retire happy in addition to writing his regular syndicated column which has appeared in places as The Edmonton Journal, Globe and Mail, National Post and many more. Jim has authored many other books including the best seller, "Mutual Fundamentals, Seven Strategies to Guarantee Your Investments and Smart Tips for Estate Planning." Most recently, Jim has developed software programs, recorded audio programs and created his new Retire Happy DVD which is a live recording of his one day retirement workshop. To learn more about Jim and his products, visit www.JimYih.com or www.RetireHappy.ca.

Co-Author: **10 Things** I wish someone had told me about Retirement

Patricia French
MSc, PRP - Financial Counsellor and
Professional Human Ecologist
Pre-retirement Educator - University Instructor
Department of Human Ecology (University of Alberta)

Don't miss this!!

The Best Retirement Plan is to be Debt Free

About Us
Corporate Introduction

Courses
(over 45 and under 45)
- 3hrs to 3 days
Keynote presentations
(1-3 hours)

Our Team
Rein Selles
Jim Yih
Patricia French

Download

Book/Products

Resources

Patricia French is a Financial Counsellor and Professional Human Ecologist specializing in planning with those who are under the age of 50. With 13 years of experience working with individuals and families, she believes financial roadblocks can be avoided or overcome with good planning. She helps families get through the rough patches, steer clear of obstacles, and get on track to achieve their financial goals. She is also a Pre-retirement Educator and a University Instructor teaching in the area of family finance. She is driven to provide participants and students with key knowledge, skills, and strategies to find their own path and safely navigate the often potholed financial road ahead.

Notes

Notes